Visual Guide to
WORKING
IN A SERIES

Next Steps in Inspired Design

Gallery of 200+ Art Quilts

ELIZABETH BARTON

Text, Photography, and Artwork copyright © 2013 by Elizabeth Barton

Publisher: Amy Marson

Creative Director: Gailen Runge

Art Director/Cover Designer: Kristy Zacharias

Editor: Lynn Koolish

Technical Editor: Alison M. Schmidt

Book Designer: Christina Jarumay Fox

Production Coordinators: Jessica Jenkins and Rue Flaherty

Production Editor: Alice Mace Nakanishi

Illustrator: Kirstie L. Pettersen

Photography by Elizabeth Barton, unless otherwise noted

Published by C&T Publishing, Inc., P.O. Box 1456, Lafayette, CA 94549

Library of Congress Cataloging-in-Publication Data

Barton, Elizabeth, 1949-

Visual guide to working in a series : next steps in inspired design-gallery of 200+ art quilts / Elizabeth Barton.

    pages cm

Includes bibliographical references.

ISBN 978-1-60705-634-8 (soft cover)

1. Quilting. 2. Art quilts--Design. 3. Serial art. I. Title.

TT835.B27557 2014

746.46--dc23

                    2013018045

Printed in China

10 9 8 7 6 5 4 3 2 1

DEDICATION
For Clare and Jane

ACKNOWLEDGMENTS

Thank you to Carol Miller and to Lynn Koolish who encouraged me to write. Plus enduring gratitude to the many welcoming and responsive people I have met since I began teaching workshops.

CONTENTS

INTRODUCTION

My first book, *Inspired to Design: Seven Steps to Successful Art Quilts*, focuses on how to be successful in designing art quilts. This book takes you to the next level—working in a series, giving you the tools you need to establish a body of work in your own unique style.

What is a series? A series is defined as a group of related objects; a series of quilts, therefore, would be several pieces that are related in one of many different ways. Obviously subject matter is one possibility, but style and format are also possibilities. Consider a series as a set of works (quilts, paintings, sculptures, even songs) related by a single theme.

Who should think about working in a series? Almost anybody who has mastered (more or less) a number of construction techniques and is ready to develop their own style. Series work is so helpful in developing design skills, construction skills, compositional skills, and expressive skills that after you are past the stage of trying out a variety of different things, a series of related pieces should be the next thing you do.

The most important benefit of working in a series is that it helps you learn how to work from your own ideas and discover your own unique voice. The quilts you make might be abstract, realistic, or impressionistic—any style you like. What develops will be your own particular style and voice. When you visit a quilt show or look at a book of quilts, which ones attract your attention the most? Which ones make you drool? What kind of paintings, photographs, sculpture, and other media do you fall in love with? Become aware of the work that excites you, intrigues you, and makes you go back to look at it again. This is the kind of work you should be making!

Looking back at my own work, I realized that I've nearly always worked in series—my very first pieces were all about windows. After that, buildings with windows, then night scenes, then roofs and chimneys, then the Red Shift series on memory (pages 18, 19, and 54), Drowned City series

(pages 28 and 29), black-and-white timbering (below and pages 5 and 6), and industrial landscapes (pages 12, 36, and 37). For me, if an idea is powerful enough to put in the time to make one quilt, I find that it is something I will certainly want to explore in depth.

Shadow with Five Diamonds by Elizabeth Barton, 26″ × 46″

Photo by Karen J. Hamrick

Strength of Quiet Windows
by Elizabeth Barton
41″ × 55″

Overture
by Elizabeth Barton
35″ × 47″

Windowseat
by Elizabeth Barton
30″ × 37″

Roof Exuberance
by Elizabeth Barton
32″ × 51″

CHAPTER 1

GETTING STARTED

If you've never worked in a series before, you may be wondering why you should be considering it. Listed below are the main reasons it would be helpful.

WORKING IN A SERIES ALLOWS YOU TO …

Develop Your Own Style

Most everything you do has a style: how you dress, what music you listen to, how you talk, how you write. Style is very individual but is consistent within the individual. Your style of making art quilts should also reflect you. That doesn't mean your style can't or won't change as you grow and learn and change. But it will still be your personal style.

Avoid Putting Too Many Ideas into One Piece

The more complex something is, the less compelling it is. An art piece should have a clear story line, and everything in the piece should support that line. Extraneous ideas don't help; they just clutter the scene. The ideas may be very good, however; so don't discard them. Add them to your inspiration notebook (page 16). When you know you can use them in another piece, you won't feel that you need to jam them all into the piece you are working on right now.

Develop Your Ideas and Technique through Practice

One of the most compelling reasons to work in a series is the desire to make better work. We all marvel when people do remarkable things with little or no apparent effort. We think it is "just luck" and that they were born with a special talent. I can't tell you how often I've heard, "Oh, I'm no good with color. I don't have that gift." It's not a gift! It's nearly all practice. Anybody who is any good at anything has practiced a lot. Libby Lehman has probably machine stitched her way to the moon and back more than once. B. J. Adams has thread painted enough dissolvable cloth to cover Mount Rushmore or the Pont d'Avignon.

More Thoroughly Explore an Idea

Too often we're in too much of a rush to finish a piece, maybe because we need it in time for a show, a challenge, or a gift. We make those early compositional decisions too quickly and feel we must hurry through the process. It feels like the world around us is always in a rush, and it's hard not to carry that over to the studio or sewing room. Implicit in working in a series, however, is the practice of exploring ideas thoroughly, looking at them in all possible ways.

Focus on One Subject

If you set the task of thinking about just one subject, then you'll be more inclined to get more deeply into exactly what it is about that subject that really interests you. This is very different from rushing from one thing to another. This is something you want to absorb yourself in, whether it is a particular city, a topic such as birds, nature's beauty, or a conceptually driven political piece protesting easy access to guns. Only when you dig deep do new ideas begin to emerge and you discover new ways of describing this theme to the viewer.

Think about the Subject's Subtleties

Focusing on one subject leads you to think about all the subtleties of your subject: not just a red flower, but a flower with infinite nuances of red, a flower that reflects light here and absorbs it there, that has soft furry surfaces and bright satiny ones, that has curving lines and straight ones, elegant parts and slightly awkward but endearing ones. It takes time and study to begin to see all of this, and even longer for you to figure out how to convey it in a piece.

Colliergate
by Elizabeth Barton
64″ × 62″

This and the next two quilts on pages 9 and 10 are from the series I made based on medieval streets. See additional quilts in this series on pages 44, 51, 79, and 80.

Broaden Your Creative Vision within Your Theme

You will find that you need to learn more ways of expressing your feelings about a theme. You will actually need to dig deeper into those feelings; instead of just liking or not liking, you'll learn to express subtleties such as how to show tenderness in stitching, gladness in color, or excitement in your line quality. The subtleties that you discover in a theme can be conveyed in so many different ways. Maybe you will need to add an idea developed from embroidery stitches to convey your deepened appreciation of your theme, or come up with some new funky way of getting dye on cloth to express the peculiarities you discover in your topic.

Perhaps you'll feel the need to learn how to show transparency in a medium that is not usually thought of as transparent; you might begin to think about cutting away the backing and incorporating transparent cloth as an overlay on opaque fabric, or find other ways to indicate light shining through a window. As you ponder these possibilities, both your creativity and your ability to express it will grow.

Working in a series leads you to explore every possible way that an idea can be expressed. Frequently the first few possibilities come very easily; but when the free flow stops and it is more work to develop the next images, your imagination and creativity get a real workout. That's the place you want to get to, because that is where the new, fresh ideas will (with luck) appear.

Coppergate by Elizabeth Barton, 38″ × 63″

Generate More Ideas

Say you want to create works about trees: The first idea you come up with might be a grove of trees, but as you think more about it, you see in your mind's eye the tender leafing out in spring, or maybe the blaze of color in fall, or the delicate tracery of winter. You might envision a closeup and detailed view such as Barbara Watler's amazing work (www.barbarawatler.com) or a faraway view to show the extent of the woods or trees in a city. Ideas soon begin to abound, and it's too much for one piece but great for a series.

When you work in a series, you need to think about different ways in which ideas can be generated. You'll explore this topic in some depth in Chapter 3 (starting on page 39) where we'll take a look at some of the traditional ways of developing designs (tracing, photographing, and so on) and some newer and less common possibilities.

Fossgate
by Elizabeth Barton
45″ × 93″

Develop Your Ability to Assess the Quality of Your Work

Learning how to evaluate the strengths and weaknesses of your work takes knowledge, time, and examples. If you have only one example of this or one example of that, it's very hard to make an overall assessment of quality. This is why most art and quilt shows like to have more than one entry—with three pieces, for example, jurors can make a much better judgment of your work. For you, too, strengths and weaknesses become much more evident when you have several examples. As you see both problems and successes, you will find yourself thinking about your work in new and deeper ways. Learning the vocabulary with which to talk to others and, more important, yourself is a vital task. Working in a series will lead you to a deep knowledge of basic design principles and then to the development of critical-thinking skills.

Develop a Body of Work

If you want to enter shows, be in a group show, or perhaps have your own solo show, and in general be taken seriously as an artist, you need a body of work. Multiple pieces around ideas or themes illustrate your focus, commitment, and dedication, which are very important in showing the quality of your work.

EXERCISE

Working in a Series—Should I?

Get started now by taking pen and paper (or keyboard and computer) and writing down just why you should work in a series. What do you want to get out of it? Print your list—make it large—and pin it up on your design wall. This is your stated goal and will help keep you on track when you might get distracted by other possibilities.

WHEN SHOULD YOU CONSIDER WORKING IN A SERIES?

You should definitely be into serial work after you've explored a number of different ideas, taken various workshops, and tried different techniques. It is the only way to focus on developing your own voice, themes, ideas, and style. Imagine that you're trying to develop a unique style of handwriting: You might try out different writing instruments (pencil, charcoal, ball-point pen, italic pen, brush), different kinds of paper, different types of written material, different sizes of letters, different writing positions, different colors of ink, and different shapes of letters. That would be fun, but how would any of those be distinctive? To develop your own style, you need to make some decisions and focus on them.

Consider committing yourself to developing at least six related designs for quilts. You can do this sequentially, working from one design to another, or you can plan the whole thing at once in one fell swoop! Working through this book and doing the exercises will help you focus on your journey.

> **tip** *But I Can't Draw*
> *Don't worry about being able to draw. Drawing is a skill that can be learned by anyone, and drawing skills improve with practice. However, you don't really need to be able to do anything other than a rough sketch to design your quilt series. Excellent drawing skills are definitely not needed! As long as you can indicate the main shapes, lines, and values, you will do just fine.*

THINKING ABOUT SERIES WORK

To get into the frame of mind for series work, consider a group of quilts related by a single idea or theme, the basis of which can be *content* or *form*. The examples that follow are an introduction to get you thinking. Chapter 2 (pages 15–38) has more examples of using content and form in series work.

Planning a Series by Content

The content is what the work is about; for example, the content of a biography would be a particular person's life, or the content of a song cycle might be songs about spring. Content can be tangible and concrete like cakes or mountains, but it can also be abstract. You could choose a theme like joy, sadness (though that might be rather depressing), nature's bounty, or more subtly, the intersection of human beings with nature.

Steelyard Frieze **by Elizabeth Barton, 68″ × 33″**   Photo by Karen J. Hamrick

Rusty Answer **by Elizabeth Barton, 24″ × 41″**   Photo by Karen J. Hamrick

Steel Reflections
by Elizabeth Barton
24″ × 18″

These three quilts are part of a series about a steelworks.

Photo by Karen J. Hamrick

Planning a Series by Form

The term *form* refers to how the work is made. In fiber art, this might be the exploration of a particular format. Grids, in all their many presentations, have been the theme for many, many quilts, both contemporary and traditional. Other artists have chosen to explore a technique such as the discharge of color from the fabric using various chemicals or the deposit of rust on the fabric. Many different surface design techniques have proved to be a popular and fertile mine of serial ideas—as can be seen from the examples shown here, which use hand-dyed fabrics, including arashi shibori dyeing techniques.

Semmerwater by Elizabeth Barton, 54˝ × 37˝

Rainy, Rainy Night by Elizabeth Barton, 60˝ × 35˝

Nantahala by Elizabeth Barton, 31˝ × 47˝

Form and Content

The following quilts (below and page 14) are all based on showing a city—the whole idea of a city all at once, with a shallow depth, all square, and all using screen-printed fabrics. Both content and form were held constant.

Chimney Tops by Elizabeth Barton, 50˝ × 40˝

Castles in the Air by Elizabeth Barton, 60″ × 65″

Time Present and Time Future by Elizabeth Barton, 61″ × 64″

Looking at Series Work

One of the best ways to begin thinking about working in a series is to examine closely the work of well-known artists in all media (quilts, yes, but not only quilts). From such study, you can gather myriad ideas about the many different ways of developing designs based on a theme or idea. Think about whether each series you look at is based on form or content.

How Long Should a Series Be?

I asked several well-known art quiltmakers how long a series should be.

Carol Taylor (page 26):
I think the Gong series with 39 quilts was very successful. They won lots of awards and are mostly all sold.

Dominie Nash (page 32):
Some series turn out to be very short, but I'm on number 37 of the still lifes and number 20 of the leaves.

Jeanne Williamson (page 30):
With the Construction Fence series, I was planning on making a few pieces but never thought I'd be doing it for over seven years and working on number 70 or higher. I just wanted to set a few parameters to work within.

Jeanne also noted that she developed side or spin-off series at the same time. Some have proven to be shorter and some may be longer than the initial series. One series can lead to another.

FINDING YOUR THEME

BEGIN BY LOOKING BACK

You have probably already made a number of quilts; otherwise I doubt you would be reading this book. So I think it's important to look back over the work you've created so far. It's helpful to do this visually rather than mentally. Copy or print photos of every quilt you've ever made onto standard sheets of paper. Make the image as large as you can, one quilt to a page. I like to keep these in a notebook binder, each one inside a sheet protector. Remember, each one has been a separate step along your quiltmaking journey—though I suspect that if you're like me, there have been a few side trips and trips up various blind alleys! Take all the images and spread them out on the floor or a large table.

Can you organize the quilts into themes? Are there groups of abstract work with small pieces, abstract work with large pieces, repeated blocks, landscapes, figurative/representational work, and so on? Are there any subjects to which you return again and again? Do any themes emerge as you look at your body of work to date? Can you group some of these images? Don't worry about the chronological order—it's not important here.

If you see no themes related to content (page 12), are any related to form (page 13)? For example, you might not have used the same subject very often, but have you explored a specific technique or way of using your fabric?

You are looking for sets. When you have grouped your images into sets, write a few words about the theme for that set. Can you see if you have already been leaning toward some specific ideas?

Sit back and consider whether or not any of these themes continue to interest you; do you feel you have exhausted that particular idea? Perhaps you worked on something because of a workshop or a friend's interest and you wanted to work together.

However, if you find yourself saying, "Hmmm, I did like those two quilts I made about the Antarctic; I'd love to do more on that"—or whatever the subject is—then make a note of it as a possible idea for a series.

What if every piece you have made is very different from all the others? Think about why that is. Maybe you are focusing on specific projects that have been designed by others, or maybe you have been concentrating on taking classes and workshops to learn specific techniques. It's possible that you have not yet explored very far, and reviewing your past work didn't lead to possible subjects for further study. In this case, I suggest you sit down with pen and paper and brainstorm all the things you are interested in. In one workshop I was teaching, I remember a lady who could not for the life of her think of a specific theme. She was very frustrated as everyone else happily got out pictures of beaches and flowers and block designs and so on. I sat down with her and we talked about her general interests, whereon she mentioned she had always been intrigued by calligraphy. This soon led to her deciding to design some quilts based on the theme of alphabets and letters.

Photo by John Barton

PICKING A CENTRAL IDEA

In order to work in a series, you must have a theme, a centralizing idea. If you make ten quilts, all about different things, using different techniques, in a different voice, they're not a series. Making them might be fun, but in terms of furthering your artistic identity and developing your own voice, it's not likely to help. It's a bit like trying to find a way up a mountain: If you explore the first hundred yards of ten different routes, I doubt you'll be very far up that mountain; but if you spend all your energy following one route, you'll be much nearer the top, especially if you have made some preliminary surveys and a plan.

EXERCISE

What Do You Like?

A good way to find out your own preferences is to pin up copies of all your favorite inspirations on your design wall. Do you see similarities between the works of different artists you like? Or a particular type of content or form to which you are drawn? Have you chosen all abstract pieces? Or impressionistic? Or realistic? Do you like bold colors, highly contrasted, or do you prefer soft, sliding analogous color schemes? Are you drawn to intricate texture? Do you like a strong graphic look? Keep on asking yourself these questions, and make a list of the type of work that sings to you.

EXERCISE

Creativity and Inspiration

Creativity often starts with a collection of inspirations—images we gather from many sources. It's very helpful to keep this inspiration in a notebook, a box, or even just a pile in an in-box. The collection doesn't have to be a fancy scrapbook, and the arrangement is immaterial. You can keep your inspiration digitally. What's important is to have these stimuli, these little triggers, to the creative muse. These days you have so many sources of inspiration: books at the library, good-quality art magazines, the Internet, and a digital camera that you should be carrying with you at all times.

If you don't already have a collection of inspirations, start now keeping images that fascinate or delight you in any way. Aim for at least 100. When you have them, spread them out on the floor and group them into themes. For example, you might have a lot of skies, trees, animals, groups of people, abstract mysterious patterns, or bold graphics. Many people like pictures of buildings; others prefer simple, natural scenes such as horizons. Look at this wonderful series by Julia Loffredo Triebes, in which she subtly alters the height of the horizon line.

Photo by Julia Loffredo Triebes

Horizon #5 **by Julia Loffredo Triebes, 30″ × 30″**

Photo by Julia Loffredo Triebes

Horizon #3 **by Julia Loffredo Triebes, 30″ × 30″**

Photo by Julia Loffredo Triebes

Horizon #4 by Julia Loffredo Triebes, 30″ × 30″

Photo by Julia Loffredo Triebes

Horizon #2 by Julia Loffredo Triebes, 30″ × 30″

Sometimes, of course, you want to make a little bit more of a shift, as Julia did when she went from black to white.

Photo by Julia Loffredo Triebes

White Horizon by Julia Loffredo Triebes, 56″ × 50″

Themes can be quirky things like umbrellas or balloons or outhouses! See Christo's wonderful umbrella installation in Japan (www.christojeanneclaude.net > Artworks: Realized Projects > The Umbrellas).

Looking at all your inspirations at one time not only will help you to get an idea of where your own personal taste lies, but also will suggest potential themes that you might want to work on. Don't forget themes that relate to form as well as to content. You might have several pictures of children (content), but you also could have picked out several images with a lot of repeated shapes (form). You could find that your pictures are all of different subjects, but they're all black and white with one other color. Or that you are drawn to images with lots of skinny lines.

After you have collected and sorted the inspirations, write a summary of your findings. The paragraph should begin: "I am inspired by …" Don't worry if you are inspired by more than just one thing.

THEME AND VARIATIONS

When working in a series, the important thing is to hold some variables constant while others vary. The basic theme, or in musical terms, the basic melody of the work, would be held constant. The variables could be in the way the melody is presented and developed. Think about classical music where the composer used a theme (Bach and Beethoven both did this) and then composed amazing variations of that melody by varying the key, the pitch, the tempo, the ornamentation, and so on. Think of a series as a return to a theme. We all have themes that we return to over and over again, for a truly interesting theme can be interpreted in so many different ways.

What is constant in one series might be the variable in another series. For example, you could take a color and vary the shapes with which you present that color. I did that with my series Red Shift. At right are three quilts from that series.

Red Shift 3 **by Elizabeth Barton, 25˝ × 35˝**

Red Shift 6 **by Elizabeth Barton, 25˝ × 35˝**

Red Shift 5 **by Elizabeth Barton, 25˝ × 35˝**

A theme can have endless variations and combinations. Everything can be flipped around and rearranged in a different way. With music, there might be variations on a specific melody or a series of compositions that are all marches with different melodies. Each would be a series, for in each, a particular aspect or element is held constant. For us, the great beauty of this is that it's possible to design a series of quilts from the starting point of content or form—whichever takes your fancy.

On the following pages are some specific exercises to help you learn more about your own taste, helping you focus in on the direction you might want to take in your series.

Take your time with these exercises; you are exploring a whole country. Don't rush, and don't dive in before knowing where you're going to get out!

Analyzing Themes and Variations

Write down quickly the names of your favorite artists in all media. Then narrow the list down to two quiltmakers, two painters, and two artists from another medium with whom you are familiar. You could choose composers, songwriters, poets, choreographers, ceramists, jewelers, embroiderers, weavers, dancers, sculptors, novelists, or even filmmakers. You are going to take a close look at their series of works, particularly the themes they work in.

If they are visual artists, you can probably find examples of their work on the Internet: print or photocopy at least six of their pieces *from one series* (many artists work in more than one series at a time). If they work in a less visual medium, make a list you can refer to, for example, a list of songs written by Bob Dylan or variations on a theme by Beethoven.

The next step is to analyze each of these artists and the examples you have picked. What do each of the examples have in common? Try to verbalize what is constant. How can you tell, for example, that a quilt is by Judith Larzelere or by Linda MacDonald? Larzelere's work is distinguished by form. She uses a particular technique based on Seminole or strip piecing. The strips are arranged in boldly contrasting directions, often diagonally; the colors are strong; and the work is abstract.

MacDonald's work is thematic because of her content. She has made many pieces about the environment and uses a black-and-white drawing tool on a neutral ground.

Look at your artists' examples closely. Can you identify theme and variations? What idea did they take, and how have they changed or developed it with each piece? Exactly what did they do? If you look at Andy Warhol's iconic screen prints, for example, you can see how he changed the color scheme on each one.

If you read a mystery writer such as Henning Mankell, it is evident that the setting of southern Sweden, the main characters, and their modus operandi remain the same, but the criminals and their crimes vary. If you look at Linda Levin's art quilts, you can see that one of her main themes is cityscapes, specifically New York City, where she lives. She changes the light, the configurations, the focal points, and the mood; but the basic theme and structure hold steady.

City with Footnotes XII by Linda Levin, 41″ × 49″

Photo by Joe Ofria

City with Footnotes V
by Linda Levin
63″ × 72″

Photo by Joe Ofria

City with Footnotes VIII
by Linda Levin
40″ × 49″

Photo by Joe Ofria

Look at the work of Jasper Johns in his U.S. flag paintings. (Search the Internet for "Jasper Johns flag" and then click on *Images* to bring up an image page full of them.) Look at each one and note the changes that he makes. Sean Scully is another painter who has made many variations on a theme. He usually works from themes derived from photographs of old doors.

Form: Using a Simple Unit

EXAMPLE 1 *Windows Series*

Beginning with a *simple unit* is a very good way to work, and I have made several series of quilts this way. My very first series was based on a simple unit or motif, but one that was very significant for me. I was raised in a dark northern city in England, and windows, the source of light, were always very important. I remember as a schoolgirl, my first thought when we moved to a new classroom was to get there early so that I could get a seat by the window. To this day, whenever I go into a house I haven't

been in before, the first thing I look for is the view from the windows. Therefore, it was very natural for me, when thinking of a simple idea for a basic unit, to take that of a window—a light rectangle surrounded by a darker frame. Oh, the possibilities, both literal and metaphorical! And here are some of the window quilts I made with explanations of how I developed the theme by means of small changes that significantly affected the mood and the overall look of each piece, thus creating a series.

Windows 1: Red Quilt **by Elizabeth Barton, 30″ × 40″**

The basic unit is a rectangle with narrower strips of fabric added to all four sides. Sometimes the rectangle is darker than the surrounding sides, sometimes lighter. A very simple motif like this can be extremely versatile. This was my first quilt in the series, and I presented the units very straightforwardly.

Windows 2: Reflections **by Elizabeth Barton, 30″ × 40″**

In the second quilt, I made several changes based on observations from my first quilt (at left). I changed the palette and added more strips.

Warm Light by Elizabeth Barton, 40″ × 60″

In this third quilt, I made several changes based on observations from my first quilt, *Windows 1: Red Quilt* (previous page). I felt I had lost some of its character when I severely squared off the top and bottom before adding the borders. So in the third piece, I made the border much more uneven. I also thought it would be fun to use fabrics with a smoky translucent effect and softer, more glowing colors. I liked the idea of lost edges and sometimes allowed similar colors or values to merge into each other

Windows: Blue Light by Elizabeth Barton, 40″ × 53″

For this fourth quilt in the series, I looked at some windows and realized that a window frame is often made up of two or even three sets of side pieces. I thought it would be fun to add these and also to repeat the idea of a skinny insert by adding a long strip between the windows.

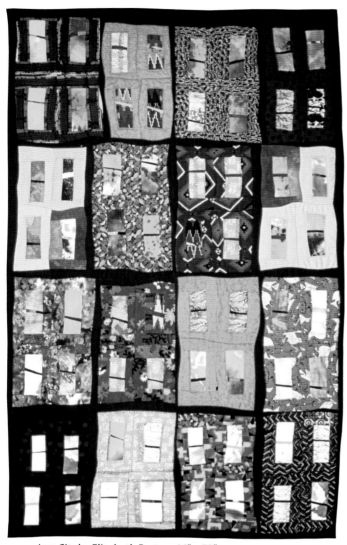

Jazz City **by Elizabeth Barton, 46″ × 72″**

Petra **by Elizabeth Barton, 45″ × 55″**

In this next quilt, I began to think about windows in the setting of a simple, small house. I had a lot of African and boldly patterned fabrics and liked the idea of warmth and friendliness these fabrics conveyed. That was so much fun that I actually then made another quilt like this, which I immediately traded for a painting!

What could I do next in this series? Having developed my first windows into little houses, I began to think of bigger buildings. In looking at some books on architecture I came up with the idea of setting the windows into a curve. I also had set myself the task of using a very different palette. I remembered the buildings carved out of stone in Petra, an ancient city in Jordan, described as "a rose-red city half as old as time" in an 1812 poem by John Burgon. The idea of a city carved out of stone captured my imagination, and I realized that although I couldn't visit it, I could take some of the colors for my quilt.

Oculus by Elizabeth Barton, 71″ × 41″

The idea of curves took hold, and I decided to try my hand at a large, curving piece, taking inspiration from a very famous building in Rome, the Pantheon. As well as curving the window motif, I also wanted to push the sense of texture between the windows and open up the top to the great, beautiful negative space of the sky.

This is the final quilt in Windows, a series of eight quilts that are now in the Hartsfield-Jackson Atlanta International Airport in Atlanta, Georgia. The series is at Gate 29, Concourse E, with four quilts on each side of the gate. (Should you ever find yourself in the vicinity, I hope you can take a look.) The challenge the architect and interior designer set was to make a piece that appeared to curve to the shape of the wall (not seen in the picture—alas, the quilts are too high up to photograph easily), which was a sort of shallow quarter moon.

Airport Windows: Dome by Elizabeth Barton, 15′ × 8′

EXAMPLE **2** *Carol Taylor's Gong Series*

Carol Taylor (www.caroltaylorquilts.com) made 39 quilts based on a simple unit she called a gong.

Carol Taylor's gong motif

Funky Motif by Carol Taylor, 23″ × 23″

Going, Going, Gong
by Carol Taylor, 20″ × 53″

In *Going, Going, Gong* Carol altered size and value to create her variation. A series often begins with a simple motif and fairly straightforward, but very successful, variations!

Sound Waves **by Carol Taylor, 52″ × 44″**

In this version, Carol took that first motif and varied it by size. She could have used color or value or proportion, but for this first variation on a theme, she opted for a simple but very effective size variation, with large motifs in the middle, medium sized on the right, and smaller on the left. In the focal area in the middle, she added another variation by splitting a large unit in two horizontally, placing half above the central unit and half below.

EXERCISE

Manipulating a Simple Graphic Idea

Now see if you can find at least two other artists who have taken a simple graphic idea and manipulated it through many different pieces. It will broaden your horizons if you don't limit yourself to quilters. Search on the Internet, at the public library, or through your own art books. See if you can find at least six examples all based on one theme. Then analyze how the theme has been varied. Did the artist change the size? The color? The texture? The proportion of some of the shapes to other shapes? Just what did the artist do?

Form: Using Texture—Arashi Shibori

As you have seen, a simple graphic motif or unit can supply a multitude of ideas. However, this isn't the only element you can work with. Many of us have been seduced by surface design, and I must admit to many hours of wonderful seduction. I particularly love the texture created by arashi shibori. *Shibori* is the Japanese word for tie-dyeing, or resist dyeing. You can manipulate cloth in many ways when dyeing it so that specific areas of it resist the dye. Each way is magical in that you don't see the finished pattern until you unwrap, untie, untwist, or unclamp the fabric at the end of the dyeing session.

Arashi shibori involves twisting and wrapping the fabric on a pole and then dipping it into dye or painting dye over it. When you open up the fabric, after letting the dye work, it's like magic. Just like unwrapping a present, you never quite know what you are going to get, and it is usually quite amazing and beautiful.

In this case, the texture of the fabric itself can be the theme for a series of quilts. I ironed and petted my fabric for some time and began to realize the patterning looked to me a bit like swirling water. If you look at the bottom of a swimming pool, you can see a restless looping pattern of shadows and light. That led me to remember the old myths and legends about drowned cities. Nature's revenge for the desecration caused by human beings in mythology has often been to drown the offending city. Many such old stories are told, including one in the Bible (you remember Noah).

Sometimes the stories imagine life continuing in the drowned cities—the cathedral bells still ring and lights glow in the windows through which the fish swim. I love the complexity of the image of a drowned city. Sometimes it's magically wonderful and mysterious, and other times it's retribution for attacks on the environment. So it was the texture of the arashi cloth that led me to my environmental (and yet strange and mysterious) theme. Below are some of the quilts from my Drowned City series.

***Arrogance of Calm* by Elizabeth Barton, 53″ × 29″**

This quilt is based on some drawings I made of St. Ives in the United Kingdom. It is pieced and appliquéd and uses fabrics that have been discharged twice using traditional arashi shibori techniques. The arashi markings give the impression of ripples, as if you were underwater swimming through the puzzle of a drowned city.

***Semmerwater* by Elizabeth Barton, 54″ × 37″**

Semmerwater was my first Drowned City quilt; I loved both the surface beauty of the idea and the rather sinister underlying possibilities.

Overlook by Elizabeth Barton, 54″ × 39″

Later in the series, even though I redefined the loopy swirls as shrubs and trees, the arashi texture remained a constant, holding the pieces together as part of the same body of work.

I have a bad habit of reading a certain meaning into everything, and thus I see something in the arashi texture, whether it is underwater, surface water, vegetation, and so on. But this particular texture can also be used in a much more abstract way. Jan Myers-Newbury has developed a very clear signature style based on her masterful use of arashi shibori arranged in geometric forms.

Photo by Sam Newbury

October by Jan Myers-Newbury, 64″ × 38″

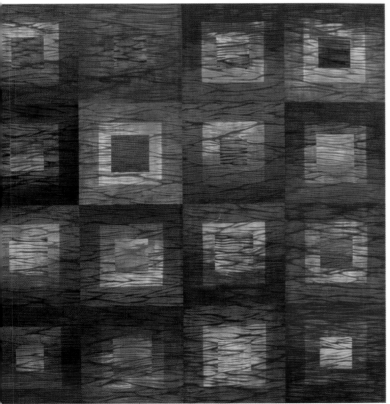

Photo by Sam Newbury

Ode to Albers by Jan Myers-Newbury, 75″ × 75″

Photo by Sam Newbury

Ten Squared by Jan Myers-Newbury, 60″ × 60″

Form: Using Texture—Monoprinting

Most artists don't plan the length of a series when they begin working on one. Their aim is to see how far a particular idea can take them. They feel it's important to push as far as they can beyond the easy or obvious responses that arise initially. I'm sure that Jeanne Williamson did not know just how far her Construction Fence series would last when she began in 2002 to use sections cut from different fences to create texture and pattern on cloth. Construction fences, which are made from brightly colored plastic, precut in various fence patterns, are used to indicate where the ground has been broken up by workers. At first the fences all seemed to be orange, but now you can see them in different colors all over the world. Because of this, the pattern creates a universal theme for both structure and disturbance, a great mix of meaning that adds to the work.

Fence 1 **by Jeanne Williamson, 31″ × 40″**   *Photo by David Caras*

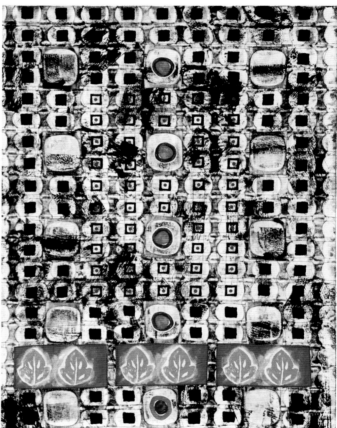

Fence 6 **by Jeanne Williamson, 31″ × 40″**   *Photo by David Caras*

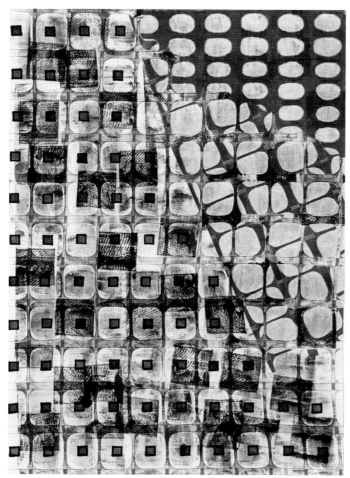

***Fence 34* by Jeanne Williamson, 33″ × 47″** *Photo by David Caras*

***Fence 63* by Jeanne Williamson, 34″ × 37″** *Photo by David Caras*

Examine closely these examples and many more on Jeanne's website (www.jeannewilliamson.com) to discover the subtle way she changes the pieces.

It isn't only fiber artists who make series based on a complex texture. Look at Internet images for the paintings of German artist Gerhard Richter. He has made artistic works in several different series. One of them is purely texture in which he develops a luscious pond-like texture of color and reflection by scraping one color over another and another and another.

Form: Using Line

Line is one of the five basic building blocks (line, shape, value, color, and texture) of two-dimensional art. It can be defined as the path of a moving point or a connection between two points. Lines are everywhere—most written alphabets are composed from lines, for example. Lines can be created by narrow strips of fabric, cord, heavy stitching, or even fabric formed into a tube or bias strip. Line can both describe an edge between two shapes and be a contour defining the limits of a shape. Line is an element that has so much room for exploration, especially in a series, because of the many different kinds of lines: straight, curved, direct, meandering, short, long, thin, thick, sharply zigzagging, or sinuous. They can be bold or hesitant.

Line is wonderfully expressive. Many different emotions can be conveyed by varying the line quality. Try drawing an angry line, then a calm line, a nervous line, and so on. They can be of any length or breadth and occur anywhere within the piece. Although line isn't as popular as shape in traditional quilts, except perhaps for string quilts, some contemporary art quilters have made amazing works using line. Many painters have used line as the basis for their series; perhaps one of the best known is Brice Marden, with his organic lines (www.matthewmarks.com > Artists > Brice Marden). Piet Mondrian (Internet search or on www.wikipedia.org) used very skinny straight lines. Both of these kinds of lines have been used by art quilters to develop series. Look at Eleanor McCain's work (www.eleanormccain.net), Eileen Lauterborn's quilts (www.eileenlauterborn.com), and Dianne Firth's work (Internet search > "Dianne Firth's APM portfolio" [www.craftact.org.au]).

EXERCISE

Using an Abstract Building Block as a Theme

Looking at all the above examples, think about how you might develop a series from these abstract building blocks (using a simple unit, using texture, or using line). Ask yourself how you could explore line in quilts or how you could work in a series involving light and shade. What other ideas can you come up with?

Content: Different Views of the Same or Similar Things

One of the most common ways of developing a series is by working with specific content. This can be something from nature like flowers, figurative work, animals, or buildings. Artist Dominie Nash has worked in several series, especially landscapes and nature, but perhaps one of her most successful series is Stills from a Life.

From an early age, Dominie was intrigued by still life paintings, especially the work of Giorgio Morandi (1890–1964). From this long-term interest she was inspired to develop a series of works based on both arrangements of objects she had made herself and also on more or less accidental arrangements discovered in daily life. One lesson here is to always keep your eyes open and your camera handy, for inspiration can be found everywhere.

Many quilts are on her website (www.dominienash.com), showing this and other series on which she's worked. Here are a few examples to look at and analyze.

Stills from a Life #35
by Dominie Nash
59″ × 48″

Photo by Mark Gulezian/QuickSilver Photographers

In this piece, repeated variations of the rounded bowl shape are contrasted with vertical rectangles.

Photo by Dominie Nash

Photo by Dominie Nash

Stills from a Life #23
by Dominie Nash
61″ × 41″

In her 23rd still life quilt, Dominie carefully balanced the items arranged on a tabletop and at the same time distorted the perspective. This makes the design much more interesting than a straightforward representation of what she saw and enables the viewer to see both the volume of the vessels and their relationship to each other.

Stills from a Life # 24
by Dominie Nash
61″ × 41″

In *Stills from a Life #24* the same plant form appears, but a different rhythm is created as Dominie contrasts depth with the plant. Interlocking paths lead from the bottom to the top of the quilt.

Photo by Mark Gulezian/QuickSilver Photographers

It's very helpful to look for series in painting, especially by artists whose work has stood the test of time. Several artists have painted a series of works based on a single view. One of the best known is Hokusai's series *100 Views of Mount Fuji*. Hokusai (1760–1849) was a much-loved and admired Japanese painter of scrolls. Several other Japanese painters of that era also worked in series; their paintings too are gorgeously composed and worth analyzing. Search the Internet for "100 views of Mt. Fuji" to see images.

The French impressionists also worked in series: Cézanne painted multiple views of Mont Sainte-Victoire in his dream of capturing the light on the mountain. David Hockney, the British artist, painted many pictures of his little dog Stanley, to whom he was devoted.

Can you think of an artist who has made a series of works based on a specific image?

Stills from a Life #37
by Dominie Nash
39″ × 58″

And in *Stills from a Life #37* the containers on the table are reconfigured, and the background is more formalized. The shapes are treated quite differently, with both volume and transparency being utilized.

Content: Nature

Themes from nature, particularly botanical themes, have always been popular with artists in every medium. Think of the amazing flower shapes by glass artist Dale Chihuly or the huge close-ups of flowers by Georgia O'Keeffe. There are so many different flowers and different ways of working with them. Plan a walk today in the gardens or woods in your neighborhood and consider all the possibilities. Don't look at just the obvious seed-catalog types of images, but consider the lilies in the field too, the daisies, dandelions, and tiny little flowers that need an artist's eye to see.

Myriad other ideas in nature also would be perfect for a series of quilts, paintings, or photographs. Think about toadstools, moths, grasses, trees, tortoiseshells, aerial views of landscape, microscopic views of cells. Look at the work of Barbara Watler (www.barbarawatler.com), who has done wonderful series of tree branches and fingerprints, and the work of B. J. Adams (www.bjadamsart.com).

Content: Time

Abstract concepts can also be used in serial work. The concept of time yields itself to many interesting ideas. I liked the idea of looking not just at time but also at my time at different hours of the day. Here are three different examples from my series on time.

Hours 1pm by Elizabeth Barton, 35″ × 37″

Hours 10am by Elizabeth Barton, 33″ × 37″

Hours 8pm by Elizabeth Barton, 36″ × 37″

Jennifer Bartlett, the famous painter, made a series of paintings about the 24 hours of the day, which was published in book form in *Air: 24 Hours*, by Deborah Eisenberg. Bartlett has often worked in series, frequently in a 12″ × 12″ block format. Her blocks, however, are painted metal panels that are arranged in grids on the gallery walls. You can find information about her and her work at www.en.wikipedia.org > search: Jennifer Bartlett.

An artist has so many possibilities for serial work with time because time itself is a serial event—hours, days, weeks, months, years. You could make a series about different activities on each day of the week, for example, or the different months or seasons of the year, different holidays throughout the year, or the light at different times of day.

Content: Narrative

A series of quilts can tell a story. Faith Ringgold's book *Tar Beach* about her childhood in New York is based on a series of wonderful painted and pieced quilts. You can visit her website (www.faithringgold.com), and the children's section of your public library is sure to have a copy of the book. Perhaps you will be the first art quilter to make a series of quilts to illustrate a story you've written.

Many people have made series of quilts about the Bible. It would be fun to take a favorite book and illustrate it; for example, I would love to do a series of quilts about the Yorkshire moors based on *The Secret Garden*, a much-loved book from my childhood. I've always associated needlework with this book because when I was in school, the nun who taught embroidery read us this book as we sewed. The quilt below is a memory of the moors and the heather.

I have made several other quilts about the moors, including *Moor Farm* and *Midwinter,* but as you can see, they are not all part of the same series.

Midwinter **by Elizabeth Barton, 44″ × 26″**

Moor Farm **by Elizabeth Barton, 38″ × 24″**

Making multiple quilts about the same topic does not in itself constitute a series. These three quilts (*From the Top*, *Moor Farm*, and *Midwinter*) use very different techniques, different shapes, different palettes, and different moods—in fact they have nothing in common other than my love of the moors. Generally speaking, a series is much more focused than a particular topic in and of itself. As you look at a series of quilts hanging together on the wall, you want to see clear relationships, repetitions, and rhythms. Working in this way will stretch you— simply focusing on a certain general topic will not.

From the Top **by Elizabeth Barton, 36″ × 45″**

What Do You See?

Put on your thinking cap and reflect on serialization. Just let yourself freely brainstorm to capture possibilities, and jot them down as you think of them. Take several days for this exercise; be as loose as you can; let ideas slip through your mind as you go through your daily life. Remember, the ideas can be abstract, impressionistic, or realistic. They can be small things or large. As I look around now, I see the shadows of the leaves on the walls (Andy Warhol made a really beautiful series of paintings of shadows); I see the rectangles of office furniture and postcards pinned up haphazardly; I see tree branches and clocks, objects and their reflections, and reflections within reflections. What do you see?

EXERCISE

Analyzing Series Work

For this exercise, go back to your analysis of the work of other serial quilters. Imagine you are writing an essay on their work. First, discuss the kind of series they chose to work in: Is it abstract or representational? Related to form or content? What specific form or content? Second, describe just how they developed the series. What were the steps they took and the changes they made? Obviously you can do this with any medium—whatever attracts your eye and engages your analytical faculties. You're trying to see the steps one should take and the decisions that should be pondered. Doing this exercise will give you tremendous insight and knowledge as to how to negotiate your own series. Don't skimp it if you really want to learn!

CHOOSING YOUR BEST FIT

You want your series to fit you well. To find out what is best for you, first look at and consider a broad range of possibilities. If you've been doing the exercises in this book, you are already doing this! It's not daunting, now, is it? It's not threatening and doesn't challenge you to be brilliant from the start. Sometimes our expectations—not the inherent difficulties of the task—lead us to fear that first step.

At the outset, the goal in making a series of quilts is to stretch yourself creatively and deepen your work. This is more likely to happen if you have an overall idea with parameters set at the outset than if you approach the task rather haphazardly. However, this doesn't mean you have to have every detail determined from the beginning—that certainly would be rigid and stifling. For example, if your series is going to be about the four seasons, it is not a good idea to have some of the seasons represented abstractly and others very literally. Keep them all abstract or all representational.

Following are three quilts I made based on an old cement-mixing plant in Athens, Georgia. As you can see, in each piece I focused in on a different aspect of the industrial plant, but I also kept constant the theme as well as some of the main shapes.

Cement Works by Elizabeth Barton, 42″ × 40″

Photo by Karen J. Hamrick

Tracy St. Silos by Elizabeth Barton, 19″ × 25″   *Photo by Karen J. Hamrick*

Elusive Beauty by Elizabeth Barton, 65″ × 45″   *Photo by Karen J. Hamrick*

CONSIDER THE DISPLAY

It's even more important to have an overall plan if you are thinking about displaying the series of quilts all together. In this case consider the relationships between them of size, color, shape, and so on. A series of large square pieces displayed in a gallery with one circular quilt would look very strange. Of course there could be very interesting ways to incorporate different shapes and sizes within the series, but it would be important to have a plan at the outset. For example, you might have four big square quilts, one for each season, along with several smaller pieces that relate to details within the seasons. This might be quite an extensive series, but one that would engage the viewer in a very intriguing way.

As you work through all these exercises, you are coming closer and closer to knowing exactly what you'd like to make a series of quilts about. Eventually you'll build up so much steam that you'll be panting to take the brakes off, leap into your studio, and start work on your own series!

EXERCISE

Thinking about Themes and Variations

Remember the inspiration notebook I recommended (page 16)? Get it out, together with a piece of paper and a pencil. Draw a rough table with two columns. The first column should be headed *Theme*—things that can be serialized, for example, trees, patterns of loops, and so on.

The second column should be *Variations*—ways in which the theme indicated in the first column could be varied. For example, if your theme is the seasons of the year, possible variations include:

- Using color alone in a very abstract way

- Using shapes such as sharp icicle shapes for winter, horizontal lying-on-a-beach shapes for summer

- Using objects such as fans for summer, rakes for autumn, and so on

Don't stop at just one way of illustrating the series. Be very specific, outlining definite parameters. Be careful to keep the ideas separate. For example, a series on trees might look at trees at different seasons or trees at different stages of growth—from acorn to mighty oak—but keep those two series separate. I've seen people make a set of four pieces where one piece interprets the theme quite differently from the other three. This is very disconcerting and leads the viewer to wonder if the series is about discord!

Don't edit at this point—just allow yourself to think freely in a brainstorming mode. Don't worry about whether or not you know how to execute a particular idea or wonder if it's been done before.

CHAPTER 3

EXPLORING YOUR THEME

HOW TO WORK IN A SERIES

After you have narrowed down your ideas to a specific theme, it's important to set some parameters regarding the variations. Whether your theme is a simple unit (page 22), a narrative (page 35), any of the other ideas described in the previous chapter, or even something completely different, it's helpful to begin with the most obvious possibilities first. This helps you center yourself and your work and allows you to gradually broaden your perspective as you look at changes, alternative views, and the development of subtler ways of expressing your ideas. Always try to give your right brain (the creative side) free rein in generating ways you can play with and express your theme.

Taking the example of trees (page 10) as a theme a little further, think about how you could develop a series of quilts based on trees. Such a series could be framed in so many ways:

- Different kinds of trees, such as oak, elm, willow

- Trees of different countries or continents

- Trees in the various seasons

- Trees in various stages of growth

- Various groupings of trees, from a lone chestnut in the middle of a field to a complete landscape covered with trees

- Various shapes, for example, anthropomorphic trees—trees as dancers or Japanese samurai

In *City in Winter*, *Three Little Trees*, and *Storm Dance* (at right and page 40), the tree is personified as a dancer and is the focus of the piece. In *Elkmont* (page 40), however, the tree theme is different—trees taking over old, ruined buildings. A subject such as trees, therefore, can yield many different series.

City in Winter by Elizabeth Barton, 26″ × 43″

Three Little Trees by Elizabeth Barton, 32″ × 18″

Elkmont by Elizabeth Barton, 51″ × 57″

Storm Dance by Elizabeth Barton, 18″ × 24″

■■ EXERCISE

Developing Themes

Take out any written material that is readily available: a novel, a reference book, a magazine, anything (well, not the phone book). Look for the first noun that catches your eye. Looking at Dickens's *A Christmas Carol*, I saw *gold*, *dogs*, *staircase*, *button*, and others.

After you have your noun, similar to the trees example, write down all the ways that the item could be addressed in a series. Obviously some ideas will work better than others, but this is an exercise in creative thinking—don't limit yourself.

SEQUENTIAL OR SIMULTANEOUS

You can work sequentially, one idea bouncing off another, but it is also possible to plan several pieces at once and work on them at the same time. Most people work on a series by making one quilt and then realizing they have another idea about that same subject. Look at the work of Nancy Crow, Kathleen Loomis, or Judith Larzelere to see how they have become fascinated with a particular form, a specific way in which the shapes and lines are arranged. Then they've gone on to make more pieces using that idea, perhaps in a different way, or perhaps more elaborate variations of their first pieces.

Sometimes when working on a quilt, you make a section that looks really great, a section that has a beauty and mystery of its own. Soon, however, it's evident that this little chunk simply doesn't go with the rest of the quilt. I must admit I would often keep that bit in there anyway. And I've definitely seen other people do that too. However, after some hefty mocking critiques from a local art professor, I realized this wasn't a very good idea. I would sadly put the inappropriate bit aside, and then I thought, Maybe this is something that can be explored in the next quilt! Although it had to be removed from the current piece, it could be used as the start for the next piece. It is like having a plant in the wrong place in your garden; the plant might be quite wonderful in its own right, but if it doesn't work well with other plants, it will attract the eye in a negative way. Better to move it to a place where it can belong.

In another quilt, you might find that you really love a particular section and want to expand upon it. *Five Mills Rampant* is actually five repeats (albeit in alternating values) of the imagery in *Flora and Ferra*.

Flora and Ferra **by Elizabeth Barton, 24" × 45"**

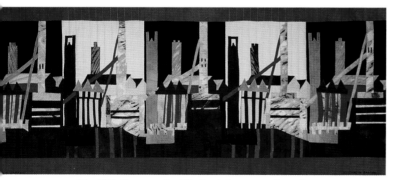

Five Mills Rampant **by Elizabeth Barton, 57" × 25"**

Carpe diem! Seize the moment! Take an idea and use it as the beginning of the next quilt. Even a small thing such as two pieces of fabric accidentally coming together on the studio floor and looking wonderful together can be a start for a piece. If this happens, pin a couple of swatches on the design wall as a reminder to use that combination. Dominie Nash tells me that while she does not carefully plan her series very far ahead, she does keep notes of ideas as they occur to her so she can develop them in future pieces. It's a good idea to keep a list right on the design wall, headed, "Ideas to be developed."

One Thing Leads to Another

Try this exercise to see how one idea can lead to another. You need pencil and paper and a viewfinder (an empty slide frame or a postcard with a 1" × 1½" hole cut in the middle). I am not going to give you any samples of this because I want you to use your imagination. You can't do it wrong. My aim is to help you get into freewheeling mode, an unselfconscious, noncritical, playful mode where the right brain works and the left brain has a little snooze!

1. Sit down, feet up, and relax.

2. Look around the room with the viewfinder, and find a little composition of lines and shapes.

3. Sketch it out, then follow the steps below; or just doodle away on a series of variations on those few simple lines. You can also do this with any simple traditional quilt block with which you're familiar.

- Sketch out your composition or block.
- Redraw and add lines anywhere you like.
- Redraw and omit lines.
- Redraw, curving the lines.
- Redraw, doubling the lines.
- Redraw a set of four of these little units together. Then try again but with one big and three little ones.

- Draw one big one and one stretched out horizontally across the top.
- Draw out in a free, loose way.
- Change to a rectangle, a rhombus, or a triangle.
- Draw out one large and superimpose one small over it, anywhere.
- Rotate through 45° and then fill in to make a full square.
- Chop it in half, separate the units, and join lines across the middle

4. Then think, What else could I do to change this little graphic?

I'm hoping that with a little practice you'll find it easy to come up with numerous variations on your starting point. This is a great exercise to do in a boring meeting—just don't make your first observation with the viewfinder too obvious!

How Many Ways Can You Use an Object?

Here's another creative activity for spare bits of time such as when in waiting rooms. It focuses on the many different ways in which a particular subject can be addressed. Try to come up with six different ways.

1. Choose one of the magazines in the waiting room and look for the first image that catches your eye—a flower, boot, cars, numbers, or gadgets—or open a book and look for a phrase or a noun.

2. Next, jot down all the possible ways that object could be the focus of a series—not just obvious ways, such as different kinds of flowers or boots, though that could be the starting point just to get your pencil moving.

Look for the subtler ways in which the series could be developed. For example, instead of ten different kinds of flowers, your theme could be ten different daisies, or ten different blue flowers, or ten different groupings of the same bunch of flowers, or ten different details of one flower.

Deciding on a Theme

Unless you are absolutely raring to go and definitely know your own mind and have your own way of working in series already established, I recommend that you give yourself time to work through all the exercises I've outlined previously. They are steps *both* in developing creativity *and* in helping you figure out what your voice will sound (or look) like.

After you've taken your time, it's time to decide upon a theme and collect as much visual material as you can in your inspiration notebook. Don't panic about whether or not you've picked the "right" theme. You can always change your mind. If you can't decide between two or three themes, choose one to start with—if you really can't decide, then flip a coin. The other themes won't go away while you explore the first one.

Developing Parameters

Every series has a theme, a central motif, a single story, a main classification. The theme is developed through multiple variations, and we've seen many ways to do this. Twyla Tharp is an amazing choreographer of many ballets and musical shows. In her book *The Creative Habit* (which I highly recommend), she describes how she develops a ballet with many sequences from a single idea. She calls that central idea the *spine* of the work. This is a great analogy because you can see how the spine holds everything together, creating unity, but also allows for many different actions, sequences, events, and so on. Obviously her events are based in movement and time, whereas art quilts are static; but the same principle of finding the spine holds. Tharp gives a lot of inspiring examples.

In the first chapter of this book I gave you two exercises (pages 11 and 14) that I hope you had time to work through. They were designed to lead you step-by-step into finding your spine—the spine you will work from and extend outward from as you develop your series of quilts. Examining other artists' themes and analyzing how they explored them should have given you much information on how a theme can be developed so you can now do it as well.

With theme in hand (so to speak) and lots of inspirational material (Tharp keeps hers in shoe boxes and has multiple shoe boxes for all the shows she has choreographed), you are ready to move ahead. You should also have written some notes about the fascination your particular theme holds for you. The next step is to develop a plan of attack—in what way will you transpose these ideas into artwork? Having a plan enables you to develop some specific parameters.

Refer to several of the quilts from the series I made based on medieval streets (page 44; many others are in my book *Inspired to Design: Seven Steps to Successful Art Quilts*, from C&T Publishing). This is an excerpt from my notes regarding that series: "I'm interested in the ways in which medieval streets wind around, in the negative shapes created by the sky, and the uneven and often cantilevered elevations of the buildings. I'm especially intrigued by how these streets look at night—the contrast of colors and the push/pull of inside/outside."

The paragraph was considerably longer, but you get the idea. Sometimes it's a bit of a jumble of notes on scraps of paper, to be honest. But I keep all those bits in one place so I can refer back to them as I develop the quilts so that I can see if I'm conveying my message. Painter Ahmed Alsoudani says, "I don't believe any artist who says 'I don't think about the viewer.'" One of the most important things is to engage the viewers, to grab their attention and focus it on the theme. That's why I like to have my notes or my paragraph to see if the piece I'm working on is going to do just that. That paragraph is important.

Let's go back to my paragraph so that you can see how I pulled out the key ideas that led to the parameters for my series: "I'm interested in the ways in which medieval streets *wind around*, in the **negative shapes** created by the sky, and the uneven and often **cantilevered elevations** of the buildings. I'm especially intrigued by how these streets look at **night**—the **contrast of colors** and the **push/pull** *of inside/outside*."

The words in italics indicate parameters or "rules." If you've taken part in a guild or group challenge, you've probably seen the many different ways a few guidelines can be interpreted (a series!). Also you can see how helpful it is to have the parameters already decided on before you start on a piece. This is one of the reasons people like challenges so much!

Goodramgate by Elizabeth Barton, 66˝ × 53˝

Haworth by Elizabeth Barton, 60˝ × 66˝

Newgate by Elizabeth Barton, 36˝ × 46˝

Zeroing in on those words in your thematic paragraph that can be interpreted visually is a way to use your left brain (the verbal side) to set up some rules or parameters with which to challenge the right (creative) side. Despite popular notions, artists, writers, and musicians rarely begin their creative work by sitting down in front of a blank computer screen, a blank sheet of paper, or a blank music manuscript. An inspiration is already floating through their heads. Writing a paragraph from the heart, not thinking, not editing, gets you into the free flow of ideas where you come up with something that is not only fresh but is also very important to you. Then you switch to the editing task, where you look for what can be illustrated in the two-dimensional visual medium of quilts. As you can see in my example (page 43), I picked out the specific words that would help to guide me in the plan for my series. I read through the paragraph and made italic the visual words. After I'd done that, I could focus my theme on medieval buildings and the actual aspects of those buildings I wanted to explore:

- Streets that wind around
- Negative sky shapes
- Cantilevered elevations
- The street at night
- High value and color contrast
- Inside versus outside

You don't want to include everything in every piece—it would be too confusing. In a series you don't have to worry about trying to include everything because you can make as many quilts as you like to explore all your ideas.

In a recent workshop one of the ladies wanted to work on portraits. I asked her to write a paragraph about portraits and what they meant to her. She wrote that the portraits that really interested her were the quilters in the workshop. She felt them to be a group of remarkable women. She also realized that she wanted to portray both a full head shot and a profile view. With these parameters she was therefore able to immediately set to work, visualizing the whole series at one go.

A theme can be addressed in many ways, so it is important to be clear from the outset how you will do this; otherwise, you can end up with a mishmash of ideas loosely linked by a particular subject, rather than a discrete, unified series. For example, if you choose grids as the main theme, you might easily make a dozen quilts that barely relate to each other because of the many possible ways of doing grids. But if you say, "I want to do a series related to grids that I see on my walk to work each morning," then the series would be quite fascinating and very personal. Or you could be more abstract and make a series of grids that had shadows—you could find these as you go about your daily life, or you could make a series of photographs of grids held in front of a white wall with an angled light source and work from those pictures. Or … or … or …!

Some themes, such as nature, are so huge that you obviously have to narrow them down. British sculptor Andy Goldsworthy works with natural materials in real landscapes; each series of works is related to specific natural materials (such as ice, leaves, or twigs in water) that he then manipulates. Being specific about the theme helps you to see a starting point. You'll probably get more ideas as you go along. Write them down and assess whether or not they fit into the current series or should be saved for a later series. Extra ideas are good—but not in the wrong place.

EXERCISE

Set Parameters and Explore the Possibilities

You may have already done this, but if not, take your paragraph and underline the key ideas as I did, shown in italics (page 43). Then examine all the research you have done on your theme. What is going to be the best way to create pieces about the theme? Look at the examples I've given and the examples you've seen from other people, and brainstorm on all the possible ways your topic can be approached. Make a list. Then go for a walk or lie in a hammock and relax (whichever thinking method is best for you) and visualize the possibilities.

DESIGN TECHNIQUES

You have the theme and the parameters. Now, how will you approach the task of coming up with some compositions? In my first book, *Inspired to Design: Seven Steps to Successful Art Quilts*, I outlined in detail several ways of working from photograph to sketch to construction. In this book I'm going to approach this task from a much wider viewpoint, not necessarily one photo leading to one sketch, because we are looking at many more possibilities and more than one quilt—many more, I hope.

Looking analytically at series that other artists have made, it is clear that *not only the subject* is held constant. It's important that the series of works also be unified to create a wonderful wholeness of ideas, a single vision. To do this, both the subject *and* the techniques should be more or less constant. You may have already developed some favorite ways of working, but it's good to explore some other techniques for deriving your designs. This is particularly important because your technique should fit your idea, and not every design method is right for every idea. It's important to have a toolbox of techniques for creating and developing a design at your fingertips. Even if you've taken loads of construction technique classes, you may not have had a chance to explore different ways of deriving designs.

When you are getting started, it really helps to take the theme plus its parameters and try out various ways of working. Not every method will work for you or your current idea, but I think you will enjoy trying out these different methods.

Tracing

The simplest and probably most popular way to draw design sketches is to trace from inspirational photographs. As you trace, whether using tracing paper, ordinary paper and a light table, or an overhead or digital projector, be sure to simplify, simplify, simplify. You do not need all the little details. In fact they often detract from the finished piece. Without them you are freer to make adjustments to the light and dark value pattern and to rearrange the big shapes slightly into a more pleasing composition. Tracing has been a favorite method of mine when designing cityscapes,

which tend to have a lot of details. The advantage of tracing paper is that it obscures the details, while the outlines of the buildings, the skylines, and the interlocking jigsaw shapes (the main things about a cityscape that fascinate me) really stand out.

Original photo for *Chimney Pots*

This is an example of a photograph I took that I found very inspiring. I love the patterns of roofs and chimney pots. This was taken in Whitby, an old fishing town on the northeast coast of England and a great place for inspirational photographs. The next step was the tracing.

Tracing of photo for *Chimney Pots*

Observe how much of the surface detail I omitted; instead I focused on the big shapes and their relationship to one another. I left out sections that did not add to the composition, such as some of the roofs on the right, and I didn't bother about any of the surface detail or decorative edges.

On the next page is the actual quilt I made.

Chimney Pots
by Elizabeth Barton
50″ × 40″

Paying attention specifically to the big shapes gave me much more freedom to explore the use of different kinds of fabric and also prevented me from getting locked down into reproducing the photograph. If you try to do that, you add nothing fresh to the image—your own creativity and personality don't come through. After you trace the photo, either discard it or, at least, hide it away where you can't see it and get too hung up on concrete details. Tracing is a very useful design technique because it forces you to look at big shapes, not little ones. Also it's very easy and low cost, especially if you have a great many inspirational photos and want to pull out the ones that will work well together. If you haven't worked this way before, try the following exercise.

EXERCISE

Tracing

Trace two or three inspirational pictures or photos:

1. If the paper on which your picture or photo is printed is not blank on the back, make a photocopy onto plain paper; otherwise, you'll also see the images that are printed on the back.

2. Use tracing paper if you have it, or just tape the photo or drawing onto a window and tape any lightweight, cheap paper over the top. After all, a window is simply a large vertical light table.

3. Mount your tracings onto plain paper (white or black) so that the design is very evident.

4. Pin them all up on the design wall so you can view them over time and weed out the awkward and boring ones.

This method of designing might work for you if your theme involves working with a series of complicated photographs. Try it and see. If you like this method, it might be worthwhile to make or buy a light table, which is simply a box with a light inside and a translucent top. These are available at most office supply and art stores. I've also made them by putting a light between two piles of books or bricks and balancing a heavy piece of glass over the top.

Sketching in Pencil

I can already hear you saying, "Not for me; I can't draw!" Learning how to draw can take time and, as with every other technical skill, requires fairly constant practice to stay proficient. But I'm not talking about the kind of drawing that involves making things look real and using perspective and such. Although the concept of perspective is very important in architectural drawing, it is not necessary for making planning sketches for art quilts. You can indicate depth in many other ways that are more straightforward and appropriate to this medium (pages 90–92). I'm talking about the kind of sketching that enables you to capture visual ideas in a fast, loose, imaginative way. The quicker you draw, the more likely it is that your sketch will show spontaneity and be refreshingly quirky. Try to draw without hesitating or erasing—sometimes this is easier if you simply keep your pencil on the paper.

While tracing is a good technique for cityscapes, sketching is excellent for simple graphic ideas that are a great inspirational source of design in quilts. Imagine that your theme is fences or gates or doorways. Take a sketch pad with you as you go about your daily life, and every time you see a fence, a gate, or an interesting door, make a quick sketch.

My sketches are rough, and not all of them would make great quilts, but they include a great variety of ideas. Some of the details would, when enlarged, make a very nice quilt. A small, quickly drawn sketch becomes fascinating when you enlarge it—you get all the little wiggles and smudges and hesitations, false starts, and overdrawn lines that add a great deal of character.

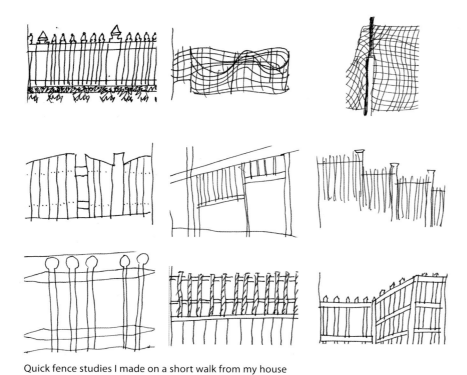

Quick fence studies I made on a short walk from my house

SKETCHING FOR DESIGN IDEAS

- The best way to find your composition is to delineate the area you are sketching either by holding up your hands in a C shape about 6″ apart or by making a little cardboard viewer—a piece of card (stiff enough so it does not flop over when you hold it up) with a rectangular hole cut in it (next page). Such a device helps you to frame the area you want to draw. Most of us are used to doing this with a camera, so we already have helpful experience of this step. Sometimes I'll take out my camera and just look through it to find an interesting composition, and then I'll sketch it.

Mount Grace by Elizabeth Barton, 75˝ × 52˝

This quilt was based on a little drawing I made very quickly while touring the monks' cells at Mount Grace Priory in Yorkshire, United Kingdom. Each monk had his own little house, and in one of them there was an old grisaille window through which the monastery buildings could be seen. My sketch, notes, and memories of a lovely day on the edge of the Yorkshire moors and a photograph of a grisaille window were sufficient.

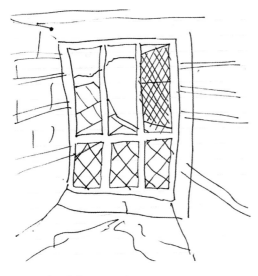

Sketch for *Mount Grace*

Viewer for sketching

- If you're looking at a landscape, it's helpful to begin with the horizon line—the line that is level with your eyes as you sit or stand. For example, if you're looking at a sea scene, the level of the sea against the sky is the horizon line, the end of the street in a street scene, and so on. After that, it's easier to focus on getting the main vertical lines first and then the main horizontal ones. If looking at three dimensions is confusing, just close one eye! That way you reduce a three-dimensional view to a two-dimensional one.

- As you draw the contour lines, don't think *boat*, *roof*, or *bottle*; think instead, *This line goes from one-quarter of the way down the left side to a point about halfway across and three-quarters of the way down the rectangle (or square).* Just think about lines going from point A to point B, like little trails on a map. Sometimes it's easier to think about drawing the negative shapes—the spaces behind things—because while focusing on them you are less likely to be distracted by the objects themselves.

- If the lines are angled, the easiest thing to do is to hold up your pencil against the view or the photograph and line it up with the angle. Then, holding your pencil carefully in the same position, mark that angle on the page. Back in the studio, you can use a protractor if you need to be more precise.

- Get the big shapes and the longest lines in place first. Details are far less important, especially in a sketch. And while it is important to consider the values, color is immaterial at this stage. It's easiest to spot the very darkest values first, so start with those. Do the darkest darks, note where the lightest lights are, and reserve those. Then look for the mediums. Do make sure you have a good range of values. If you look at the very best art quilters you will see a great value range in all their major works.

Sketching

If you haven't sketched much, review Sketching for Design Ideas (page 48). Then with pencil and pad in hand, try some quick sketches. If your theme is buildings, go downtown; if it's people, go to the market square or the mall. For animals, visit the zoo, the park, or the humane society. If your theme is going to be still lifes (arrangements of objects upon a table), then begin with a very simple arrangement of three boxes. Arrange them together on a table where you can sit on all four sides (not at once of course!). Do a sketch from each of the sides. But only take five minutes! This is not a drawing, but simply a sketch.

If your theme is abstract, you're lucky! You can go anywhere and look for arrangements of shapes and lines that seem interesting.

Wherever you go, draw quickly. Take only a small sketching book and a pencil. You want to capture just the main lines, and you want to observe what is around you, translating it into two dimensions. This educates your artist's eye immensely. It's hard to really *see*; usually we just glaze over things, making sure we don't trip as we rush from one point to another.

If you find this sketching exercise helpful, you might want to think about taking drawing lessons. Drawing is a basic skill that underlies many art mediums. It's great to be able to make an accurate pencil sketch that will give you a plan to follow for your quilt. Sketching is a great tool for developing a series because you can *move* things so easily when you sketch, arranging or rearranging the composition as you please. Sketching has an advantage over a camera because a camera can be overinclusive. The camera doesn't have the brain that you do. You can decide what to include and what to leave out—with the latter being the most important. Making quick sketches is a creative process of both selection *and* synthesis, for we are constantly observing our response to the image we're drawing and *adding* that response to the actual image as we sketch it.

Sketch for *Shambles*

Shambles by Elizabeth Barton, 38˝ × 70˝

The sketch for *Shambles* was based on a photograph and a memory of the old street called the Shambles in York, United Kingdom. I was there on a November afternoon, and it was already half dark, very cold, dank, and gloomy, but all the windows were lit up and the interior scenes looked warm and welcoming. At first I made the quilt top exactly as I drew the sketch. When I looked at it on the design wall, however, I saw that I had not included the turns and twists and mysterious dark corners of the medieval street (remember my design parameters, page 43). Drastic measures were needed! I took a photograph of the quilt top and then cut it into six vertical strips and rearranged them until I got the effect I wanted. With this plan clear, I then cut the quilt top into the same strips and sewed them back together in the new way. Much better! This was a very dramatic solution to the problem, but it worked so well that I would definitely recommend it.

Of course this story has several morals. If I had made some notes about my feelings about the mysterious medieval twists and turns of the old streets before beginning, I would have been able to assess my sketch to see if that feeling were conveyed. But, that is how we learn: doing things wrong, correcting, and then telling other people so that we remember it next time.

I've shown all these examples so that you can see that a quick, crude sketch is all you need to design a quilt. The drawings are exactly what I worked from to make the quilts. I didn't have any giant cartoons or any more detail than what you see. I know the sketch method works.

Sketching in Watercolor

Watercolor sketch for *Castle Loch*

Castle Loch **by Elizabeth Barton, 57″ × 38″**

The plan was simple. But once I start working with the fabric, all sorts of textures can be developed. For this piece I had a lot of transparent fabrics overlaying some silks and satins. As the basic structure is very simple, all the textures and overlays hang together well, and the structure of the piece is not lost. I am happy to say the quilt took Best of Show at Art Quilt Elements in Philadelphia some years ago.

Another method I like is working from a watercolor because it is such a loose, relaxed medium that the ensuing design is also quite free, airy, and painterly. Details are unimportant; the major shapes and the balance of light and dark prevail. It's also a good method for presenting ideas for a commission. Furthermore, the texture of the watercolor painting is somewhat similar to that of the hand-dyed fabric, not solid color, but color with soft, mottled variations—beautiful.

When I've decided which of my watercolor sketches I will use for a quilt, I usually find it helpful to make a value study in just black, white, and gray before I get to work. You can either make a quick pencil value study; scan the watercolor into Photoshop or Photoshop Elements (or similar photo-editing program) and desaturate to get rid of the color (page 82); or photocopy it in black and white. Doing this helps you to assess the value pattern and make sure the balance of values is both good and interesting. It's much more harmonious if one value dominates: a lot of one value, a medium amount of another, and a small amount of the third—usually the small amount will be a very light or a very dark value that you will use near the focal point to give a high contrast to that area.

Another reason to desaturate is to prevent yourself from getting totally locked into trying to match the sketch colors. Of course you may sometimes want to use the real colors because that was your inspiration, but it is often both more imaginative and relevant to choose the colors separately, reflecting your mood or your feelings, or for more formal compositional reasons. So, choose the colors last to prevent the quilt idea from becoming too literal and concrete.

Watercolor is fast and loose, so you can produce a number of different ideas or variations on an idea in a very short time—much quicker than when working in fabric.

Watercolor sketches for *Waterlilies*

Waterlilies
by Elizabeth Barton
50˝ × 31˝

Waterlilies was for a commission, and the clients had specified that they wanted a number of things included in the piece: lots of blue, water, flowers, hills, and plants. I was able to give them several different little watercolor sketches with those elements from which they could choose the one they liked the best. In watercolor you can work out most of the design, value, and color problems very quickly.

One of my most successful quilt series was called Red Shift (additional quilts are on pages 18 and 19). The *red shift* is the name for the phenomenon of light shifting toward the red end of the spectrum as it travels through time. I liked this idea to represent the idea of memory; as we look back over time, our memories shift and change from the original reality. So for this series I laid out some parameters: the color red, squares in window shapes, arranged in rows, with varied lighting emphasizing some areas of drama; and in terms of form I wanted to use the many little quilt units I stitched by hand while thinking about old memories.

Watercolor sketch
for *Red Shift 2*

Red Shift 2 by Elizabeth Barton, 83″ × 61″

Inspirational watercolors

On the Latch was a little quilt based on a watercolor of a doorway. I'd painted a number of these mainly in grays and blue grays. I loved the close harmony of the colors with a few little golden highlights. My initial inspiration was the watercolor; I didn't have the idea of working with gray fabric at all until I was inspired to start dyeing as many different grays as I could because of those watercolor paintings.

The watercolor sketch can be very simple, but it helps you to decide where the main shapes will be and how you will relate them to one another. In fact, the simpler the better, as then you can assess the balance of large shapes and also the positive versus negative space relationships.

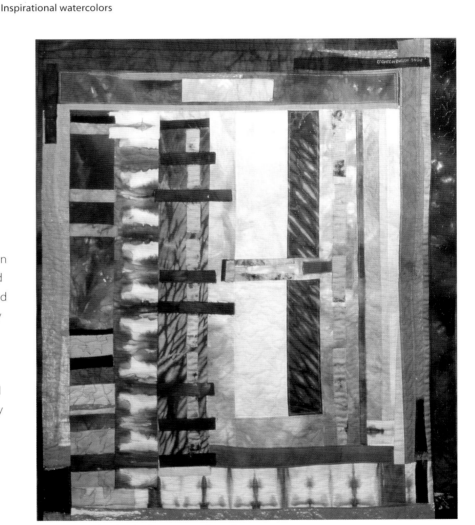

On the Latch by Elizabeth Barton, 34″ × 40″

Watercolor Sketching

Watercolor sketch of iris

Watercolor sketch of rose

Try this easy exercise to see if watercolor sketching would help you design your series. It's always good to begin with something simple. This little quilt is just a simple grid of colors at first, but if you squint your eyes or look at it from across the room, you'll see a bright flower.

A child's beginner set of watercolors will work fine for this exercise.

1. Paint a flower or tree shape against a plain background. The watercolor paint will flow readily across the paper and help you to be very loose. One of the problems with many designs is that they are way too tight. Watercolor is a great way to loosen you up. Use concentrated paint with a medium amount of water and a big brush. Be bold. You are welcome to copy my flowers or paint your own. The beauty of the watercolor is that your flower would never look like mine. It will always show the mark of your hand. Work quickly so that you can stay loose; you might find it is better to stand up and hold the brush by the tip at arm's length. A big brush loaded with luscious color will make your sketch much freer than it would be with felt-tip pens or colored pencils.

Dash off at least four versions of your flower; for example, try variations using four different colors, different numbers of flowers, or different arrangements of the light on the petals.

Poppy (in process)
by Elizabeth Barton
30″ × 30″

2. After the paint is dry, add a grid to the painting. Make as many divisions as you want according to how big you want the fabric version to be; for example, if you have a 6″ flower, I suggest you draw your grid every inch. You could paint the flower (or whatever subject you choose) onto a grid, or you could draw the grid afterward over your painting. Either way is fine, but try both so that you can see which works best for you. Then photocopy the painting in black and white, or scan it into a photo-editing program and desaturate.

3. Beginning in the top left corner, look at each square of the grid to decide if it is mainly dark (D), mainly medium (M), or mainly light (L), and write the appropriate letter on the square itself (or you can draw a separate grid). Then choose fabric where you have light, medium, and dark of the same color. Cut squares (of whatever size you've determined will work best for you) and, following the value pattern, arrange them as indicated by your painting. Again it is easiest to start at the top left corner. If you have a square that is

50/50 dark and light you can look for a fabric that has that same combination, you can join two half squares together, or you can simply make a rule that all 50/50s go to the darker color. Then sew. Fun, and it works!

This is just one of many ways to use watercolor to design your series. You can make a direct translation from the watercolor to an appliqué design as I did with *Waterlilies* (page 53), or you can try something such as the flower idea simply by superimposing a grid.

Collage

Collage is the art of cutting or ripping paper or cloth (or anything really) into small pieces and then arranging them. For the next exercise, I suggest you cut or tear paper from magazines (advertisements often have great colors and textures). You could also paint your own papers or use old paintings or photographs that you print. And then there's all that junk mail, not to mention wrapping paper or anything else that you can cut. Not only is it fun, but it's also much easier to be freer in tearing up bits of papers than it is cutting into expensive fabric.

Lavender Gothic is an example of a quilt I made from a collage using some of the images I like to play with: houses, trees, and fences. In the collage (below), I cut those shapes from magazine advertisements and then arranged them on a page and glued them down. Then I used the collage as a plan for the quilt.

Lavender Gothic by Elizabeth Barton, 32″ × 45″

If I am going to make a quilt from a collage, I mark the inches along the side of a study such as this. Each inch on the sketch represents a specific number of inches on the quilt. As this collage was quite small, each inch was translated into seven inches when I made the quilt.

I find it helpful to locate the horizon line and the vanishing point so that I can establish the angles of the houses more or less accurately. However, do remember that only architects really need to have accurate perspective; artists have much more license.

Original collage of magazine advertisements for *Lavender Gothic*

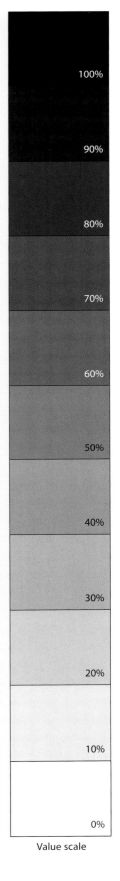

Making a Collage Design 1

1. Choose a picture from your inspiration stash, notebook, shoe box, or whatever you are using. If you have fabric you'd like to use, then make a color photocopy of it and include that too.

2. Gather the following materials. Access to a photocopier is also helpful.

- Magazines with lots of pictures, or pictures or photographs that you can cut up

- Paper scissors

- Card stock to use as backing paper (any size)

- Glue or gluestick

3. Go through the magazines, pictures, or photographs and cut out photographs. Trim away any written material (unless it is part of the image). The subject matter of the images doesn't matter.

4. When you have a nice big pile, sort the images into as many *values* as you can, putting them into boxes, trays, or plastic bags to keep them sorted. Initially this might just be three values (light, medium, dark), but as soon as you're comfortable with three, move up to five (light, medium light, medium, medium dark, dark), and so on. It's a great skill and very valuable to be able to easily see different levels of light and dark, and you will definitely improve with practice. You will also improve your value sense by photocopying your collage pieces, your inspiration pieces, *and* your fabric in black and white; then it becomes fairly easy to see and match the different levels of value. I strongly suggest that if you haven't done an exercise such as this before, you photocopy in black and white the inspirational picture from which you're going to work this exercise.

5. Determine the value of the background or most distant piece of your inspiration photo and cut or tear paper in that value. It might be easier to use construction paper for the background, or you can paint a piece of paper with gray paint in the right value. Place the background down on your base card stock.

6. Gradually work forward, cutting, snipping, or tearing the images. You can be very precise or quite loose. Either is fine; it just gives a different look. I like to get all the papers cut and arranged before I glue anything down. When you are arranging, think about the composition. Don't keep looking back at the inspiration photo to copy it exactly. That's not the point of the exercise at all. The reason for the exercise is to make a nice design using cut or torn papers, and you might need to move a shape or line or two to get the balance or the focus of interest just right. Once you start working on a piece, it's the piece, *not* the inspiration, that determines where your next shapes go.

When everything looks good, glue it down. Mount it on a piece of black construction paper, put it in a sheet protector, or even put a little mat around it to frame it. Then pin it to the design wall and stand back and look. What do you think? How do you like your design? How did you like this process? Did it help you to loosen up and move toward your own ideas and away from those of others?

> **tip** *For this exercise it's necessary to understand the importance of* value—*how light or dark something is.*

100%

90%

80%

70%

60%

50%

40%

30%

20%

10%

0%

Value scale

Making a Collage Design 2

For your second collage-based exercise, make a piece that is more conceptually based. This time, instead of working from an inspiration photograph, work from the collage materials themselves. Look at the images you've cut out and see if you can find a recurring theme. It could be cars, vegetables, square things, a particular color such as lime or violet. Maybe you love polka dots, or you could be drawn to specific calligraphy or text. What's interesting is that you were the one who chose those magazine pages to tear out or those personal photos to be cut up. There must have been something in them that attracted you, and to quite a large extent, your choices will reflect your own personal taste and interests. You're looking for elements (whether shapes, lines, colors, or textures) that you've picked out over and over—commonalities. Trim the collage materials into squares or rectangles (regardless of content) so that you can fit them together easily into a grid-like design. Then glue down.

Reassess: What do you think about collage? Did you have fun with these two exercises? Might this be a good working technique for your series?

Y/m Collage 1 **by Elizabeth Barton 26˝ × 26˝**

I made *Y/m Collage 1* from silk, following a collage of magazine advertisements fairly closely. I had cut out an office building from one advertisement, the side of a car from another, a fence from another, and so on.

I liked my little collage and thought it would be fun to play with it some more. I had recently screen printed some fabric that I thought might work with it. I put the fabric onto the photocopier so as to make some paper that had that same texture. Then I cut up the first collage and added in some strips of the screen print to make a new paper collage upon which I based the second quilt.

Y/m Collage 2 by Elizabeth Barton, 33″ × 25″

This quilt got Best of Show in a mixed media art show, which then led to a solo show in a nice gallery. You never know!

Photocopying

It's good to explore several different ways of creating designs, especially when the creative well seems a little dry. I've described several, but there are many more. I like working with a photocopier, and there are lots of different things you can do with it. Maybe you can come up with something different?

REDUCING MIDTONES

Take advantage of the photocopier's tendency to gradually reduce the amount of midtones. If you keep photocopying a black-and-white photocopy and then photocopying that copy and so on, it will begin to break down: the midtones disappear, and the images become much simpler. Strange little blobs will appear, as if from outer space, especially if you enlarge at the same time. Try it!

Image photocopied many times

When you are recopying, the details disappear, and the main masses or shapes become more evident. Since it's very important in composing to get the big shapes well defined *and* balanced in an interesting way, photocopying like this really helps to get you started.

MAKING VALUES MORE APPARENT

Photocopying in black and white is also really useful in that it makes the relative values so clear. Saturated colors can be so deceptive. I remember a quiltmaker showing me a piece where there was a very dominant bright red, but somehow the design looked unclear and disorganized. She then dimmed the light in the room and we squinted our eyes, and the intensely saturated red section totally disappeared, leaving a mishmash of medium values. Then we could see why the piece just wasn't working as a composition. Knowing your values is paramount.

Compare these pictures of a watercolor.

Quiet Neighborhood, watercolor

In *Quiet Neighborhood*, I was particularly interested in the bright light and deep shadows under the trees. But I felt that the first picture wasn't quite right. When I photocopied it in black and white I could see why—the values were wrong. They didn't bring out my theme. I then did the value study so I could see just where and how dark the darks should be; then I repainted the piece and it was much stronger.

ENLARGING

You can also enlarge when photocopying. And enlarge the enlargement and so on, ad infinitum. Then you can cut up the copy and rearrange it to get all sorts of ideas.

Look up Ellsworth Kelly's painting *Brushstrokes Cut into Forty-Nine Squares and Arranged by Chance* on the Internet for a wonderful example.

COLLAGING WITH A COPIER

Use the copier to create glueless collages: Arrange fabric or paper pieces on the glass plate, beginning with the foreground and ending with the background. Then copy.

While it's a lot of fun to do this randomly, you actually do get better results with some prior thought and organization. I suggest you control some variables while allowing others free rein. For example, you could control the shape (a square) but put as many sizes of squares as possible onto the plate.

See the above right example of doing just that with arashi tie-dyed scraps.

Copier collage with small fabric pieces

Playing with a photocopier is another way of freeing you, of enabling you to come up with ideas in a way you have not used before. You're not second-guessing yourself, and this can lead to some unexpected and original possibilities. You can take the same few elements, rearrange them in many different ways, and then look at your copies and decide which ones are most interesting and why.

EXERCISE

Photocopying for Design Ideas

Try some of the above ideas or make up your own—it's in the doing that you learn. I'm sure that as you do these, you'll think up more, and probably better, possibilities on your own.

Photographing

The camera is a great tool. Many artists begin with photography these days. Good art begins close to home—events, people, and places that have very important meanings for us personally and things that we see around us that others don't see. Always keep a camera in your pocket.

EXERCISE

Take a Field Trip

You've already decided on your theme, so now I suggest you make some field trips with a camera and try to find good examples. Imagine your theme is age or the effect of time. What might you find going out with your camera?

- Obviously old things: people, trees, buildings, furniture

- Used things: old books, used car lots

- Discarded things: car scrapyards, dumps, graveyards

- Layers of advertisements peeling off a wall and other layered remnants such as patches on clothing

The theme could be travel. Instead of just a few vacation photos, begin your travel story with packing suitcases, taking a taxi to the airport, and so on. You could do this very abstractly as well as realistically.

EXPERIMENTING WITH YOUR CAMERA

A camera can be used in many ways, not just to take a picture of something that is actually there. It's a lot of fun to experiment with mysterious effects. Some artists focus on color rather than shapes. Look up on the Internet Joy Saville, Emily Richardson, and Bridget Riley.

I do not know how these artists arrived at their images, but you can explore using just color with a camera if you blur the image by changing the focus or reducing the number of pixels. But there are other ways too: I often take pictures with my ordinary little point-and-shoot camera, and I put several layers of silk organza, plastic film, wavy glass, and other things over the lens to distort or blur the images. In the old days photographers used Vaseline on the lens to soften the image.

I love work that has some mystery to it, and playing with a camera in this way is a good place to start. The beauty of a digital camera is that it costs nothing (but time and patience) to try all kinds of different, wacky ideas. Let yourself get into a free-flow, right-brain mode and head out with an eye for distortion and obfuscation!

Back in the studio, review the images thoughtfully, looking for the ones that show the essence or spark that caught your eye. You can certainly devise a whole series of quilts based on photography such as this. Put the best pictures up on the design wall to see which continue to intrigue after a few days or weeks. If they become boring, there is no point wasting a lot of time on making a quilt based on them.

Also it's a good idea to evaluate potential quilt design pictures for a strong composition underlying the blur of color. Do you see a good and interesting structure to the value pattern? Do you see some dynamic movement? Does it have a focal area that your eye returns to after having explored most of the piece? Does the rest of the photo support that focal area? Does everything hang together? You don't just want a mishmash of color—that would look like a pile of … well, you know what!

Below is a picture of a quilt I based on a photograph of a garden through an old grisaille window.

A camera can also be used to find out hidden secrets, views no one else has noticed, things such as shadows, edges, or reflections.

Diamond Pane by Elizabeth Barton, 51″ × 73″

How about photographing:

- at night?
- through a window with rain streaming down?
- underwater (if you have an underwater camera)?
- the shadows on the bottom of a swimming pool?
- the movement of the surface of water?
- moving objects or by moving the camera (if you can disable the image stabilization)
- unusual angles, such as by crawling underneath and behind things?

Don't think in terms of mistakes, but think, How can I use the camera to make something new and strange? Try putting it very close to the object or underneath the subject of your study. You can place meshes (and yes, fingers) over the lens, you can put the camera up to the hole in the fence, you can press the wrong knobs at the right time, or vice versa.

Using Photo-Editing Software

Many, many different photo-editing programs are on the market, so I'm not going to give specific instructions for any one program—that would require a workshop in itself. Suffice it to say that messing about with images on the computer, whether they are photographs or drawings, is fun, easy, and liberating. You don't feel as if you're risking anything because you are just playing around with pixels. It also helps you to view your subject matter much more objectively and quickly. Plus, you can create many variations and changes and then compare them.

- **Adobe Photoshop** is a classic program if you have access to it. However, it is very expensive and does a million times more things than you need in manipulating designs.

- **Adobe Photoshop Elements** is a smaller, much less expensive program. It is easy to use and has pretty much everything you need. You can often download a free trial version to see if you like it. The trial is good for only 30 days, so download it when you are ready to use it.

- **Corel Draw** is a program from www.corel.com.

- **GIMP** (GNU Image Manipulation Program) can be used for painting or photograph adjustments. It is available from www.gimp.org as a free download.

- **Paint.net** has some special effects. It was developed by students as a senior design project and has been continued by them with support from Microsoft. It is available from www.getpaint.net as a free download.

Note: I have not personally used GIMP and Paint.net; all were well reviewed on the Internet.

If you don't have any photo-editing software, I suggest you do some online research to find which will suit you the best. The next step is to use it—software is only as good as your experience with it. Computer software does not create inspiration by itself. You have to be part of the equation: your observations and your imagination, plus your experience, thoughts, and feelings. What the programs do help with, however, is to give you a way of creating many different versions of the original idea, which is ideal when you are working in a series.

Don't be in so much of a hurry that you get frustrated or limit your possibilities. Be prepared to spend some time learning the software, playing with it, printing results, and putting them up on the design wall to mull over. Below, I'm going to describe some fairly basic steps to get you started.

ALTERING DIMENSIONS

It's amazing how different an image or a sketch can look if you simply alter the ratio of the horizontal to vertical measurements, changing rectangles into squares, and vice versa.

Sketch of St. Ives in Cornwall, United Kingdom, based on a photograph I took some years ago

Same sketch with ratio of height to width adjusted

Isn't the difference amazing—the whole feeling changes. Changes such as this, plus changing the colors and the values, will give a whole different mood to a piece. And so the series grows.

ROTATING AND FLIPPING/MIRRORING

Sometimes a simple thing like flipping an image horizontally or vertically will change the look quite dramatically. The focus is thrown on a different area, and the diagonals have a different impact. This function is often found on the program's *Image* menu; select *Rotate Image* or *Rotation* and then select *Flip Image Horizontally* or *Vertically*.

The following quilts are variations based on the St. Ives sketch (page 67). My main theme was that of the fascinating patterns created by roofs and chimneys flattened together into a jigsaw-type pattern.

Photo by Karen J. Hamrick

A New Day
by Elizabeth Barton
55˝ × 26˝

This was the first quilt I made from the sketch. I wanted to give the impression of early morning, soon after dawn, with hope in the air.

Photo by Karen J. Hamrick

Glow of Expectancy
by Elizabeth Barton
55˝ × 30˝

For this second quilt, I altered the horizontal orientation (*Flip Horizontal*) so that what was on the right is now on the left. This makes landscapes look surprisingly different. I also changed both the dominant color and the value pattern; I was thinking more of a warm evening mood.

Jaunty Ladies
by Elizabeth Barton
45″ × 27″

This third quilt focuses on the chimneys that I imagined to be like ladies setting out for an evening's fun all dressed up.

INVERTING VALUES

Changing values also creates a very different mood. With most of the basic photo-manipulation software you can reverse (or invert) the values, as you can see in the next two images. In Photoshop, simply use Ctrl+I to get the following effects:

Original sketch of mill buildings

Sketch values reversed

CUTTING, MOVING, AND PLACING

You can cut out sections of an image and move them to different places. You can do this with a sketch, a photograph, or the actual pieces of fabric before they are sewn together, but it's easiest on the computer using photo-editing software. It's very easy to cut and move, duplicate, or flip sections of your idea. You can even take a photograph of a piece that is already sewn together and then virtually cut it up and rearrange it to see if a different arrangement would have worked better.

Here are two of the many possibilities I considered for a recent piece, *Pond through the Trees* (below). You can see how I just cut and moved one section of the image to see if I liked it better elsewhere. Later I cut a whole strip off the bottom and made it vertical, which I liked much better and finished the quilt with several vertical elements.

First try

Second try

Pond through the Trees **by Elizabeth Barton, 50˝ × 30˝**

Know Your Size and PPIs

If you are going to slice up images and repeat them or join new ones together, it is important to decide image size and pixels per inch (PPI) at the outset. This is because when you move the images to a *New Page,* you want them to fit correctly onto that page and to be consistent with each other. Each page can be set to a specific size in inches or centimeters and a specific PPI. If you have your image at a different PPI from the page, the image will be either too small or too large on the page. I have found that 100 PPI is an easy number to remember and to work with; it is not too large and not too small. Of course you can choose whatever resolution you want—just make sure that the resolution of the images you are going to move is the same resolution as the page to which you will be moving them.

If you make a mistake and forget to match size, it will be immediately apparent. Just use *Edit–Step Backward/Undo* to erase any mistakes, and no one will ever know. That is the wonderful thing about computers; they patiently let you make the same mistakes over and over again!

Every time you move something onto the *New Page* or add text, it creates a layer. When you have your new composition all arranged, consider flattening using *Layers—Flatten Image.* If you do not flatten or merge the layers, they are stored in your image file as single layers. This is helpful if you think you might want to come back at some point and change one of the layers, but it makes a very big file, so the program will usually prompt you by asking if you want to merge the layers. Merging does not affect the *image* size; it affects the *file* size. A merged image is just one layer; a nonmerged image includes every layer separately. You can see all of the layers in the *Layers* toolbar. In some versions of photo-editing programs, you must select the correct layer to edit it.

If you are unsure about any of this, try it both ways and see for yourself what difference it makes. It is always good to play with all the items in the menu to see what happens.

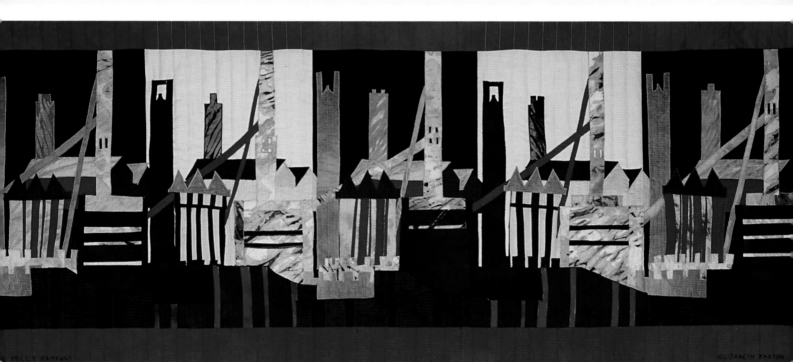

Photo by Karen J. Hamrick

Five Mills Rampant
by Elizabeth Barton
57˝ × 24

This quilt is made from a design where I alternated value changes with five repeats.

SCAN, FILTER, FLIP, RESIZE, CUT, MOVE

After sketching a design and scanning it into the computer, I use several different filters to change the look of the sketch. Some of my favorite filters are *Cut Out*, *Poster Edges*, *Photocopy*, and *Watercolor*. However I strongly recommend that you take a simple image and then look at it with *all* the possibilities in the *Filter Gallery* or whatever your photo-editing program calls these manipulations. Make a note of your own particular favorites. Some of them will suggest a definite direction to follow; others may just set you off thinking and imagining. But all will give you a different perspective on things.

For my quilt *All That Glitters Is Not Gold*, I flipped some versions of the sketch horizontally and kept some small ones and some larger ones. Then I opened a *New Page* and arranged my images on it. I also played with the *Opacity* so I could overlap images and still see both sketches.

Oil pump sketch for *All That Glitters Is Not Gold*

Experimenting with Photo-Editing Software

You've seen some of the ideas I've tried. Now, scan in a simple sketch, make all the changes I've described, and then start exploring on your own. Look at all the filters you can use and make an example of each one. Playtime! Very often the simplest manipulations are the best. While your software may have many filters and effects you can play with, you can create lots of variations with the simple combinations I have described—perfect for creating a series.

All That Glitters Is Not Gold by Elizabeth Barton, 40˝ × 18˝

Photo by Karen J. Hamrick

CHAPTER 4

DEVELOPING YOUR SERIES

You've picked your theme, you've explored different ways of coming up with design ideas, and you've decided upon the best designs. And now to work! As you work, however, you will find yourself wanting to delve more deeply into how to make your work stronger and how to communicate your feelings and intentions more clearly. What are the best ways to unify and support a design? How can you make the underlying value pattern really work for you? What are the pitfalls in working directly from a photograph? What if the quilt doesn't look as good as you hoped when you took the photo? How can you make your landscapes richer and more believable? When you're working in a series, these are the kinds of questions you find yourself wanting to answer. This is the great beauty of serial work—instead of just skimming the surface of quilt design, you're ready to tackle the problems with much more knowledge and with more elegant and unique solutions. In this section of the book, you'll dig deeper into these design tasks—above and beyond the usual beginner lessons in design.

INTUITION

As you begin to work on your series, many composition and design issues will come up. Instead of gazing for hours at a piece wondering why it's not working, it's helpful to seek the answer analytically. The more knowledge you have and the more you practice using it, the more you will build up your intuitive resources. Intuition is based on knowledge so ingrained through practice that the response feels automatic. Intuition doesn't come from the air around you; it comes from your own thoroughly researched and practiced knowledge of the subject. There are so many factors to take into account in art, and it's difficult to learn and apply them all at once. I suggest you read through the ideas in this chapter and note the ones you think will help you most.

UNDERLYING STRUCTURAL PATTERNS

To achieve a good composition, especially a unified one, it is helpful if the design of the quilt has a strong basic structure that holds everything together, ensures it is in balance, moves the viewer's eye around, and creates movement and countermovement. The structure is the underlying arrangement of the main shapes and divisions in the quilt. Art books describe such structures in a number of different ways, such as letters or geometric shape:

- Letter shapes such as S, Z, U, or L, meaning that the important elements (shapes, values, and so on) fall into an overall shape that looks like a letter of the alphabet

- Horizontal, such as a landscape or a seascape

- Vertical , such as buildings, a cityscape, or forests

- Radial/nuclear, radiating out from or into the center of the quilt, as in a traditional Lone Star pattern

- Pyramidal, where the center element is much higher than supporting side elements, often found in portrait pieces with one predominant figure

- Jigsaw, where the pieces fit together either geometrically if the area of the quilt is divided up into squares and rectangles and so on, or a more free-form, organic way where shapes interlock with one another

Estuary I by Elizabeth Barton, 31″ × 43″

In *Estuary I* the horizontal structure helps create the feeling of a flat, watery landscape, while the vertical elements give sufficient contrast to prevent the quilt from being boring. In *The Beach in Winter* (page 77) the horizontal structure is again used to demonstrate the wide expanse of the quiet winter beach.

Tower Blocks by Elizabeth Barton, 39″ × 39″

The underlying grid structure in *Tower Blocks* helps to control the somewhat top-heavy feeling that such buildings create.

April Rains by Elizabeth Barton, 56″ × 29″

The basically horizontal plan emphasizes the buildings lined up along the stream. If *all* the lines were horizontal, however, it would be boring, so the vertical and diagonal lines provide contrast.

Following are more examples of different structures that are very common in art quilts.

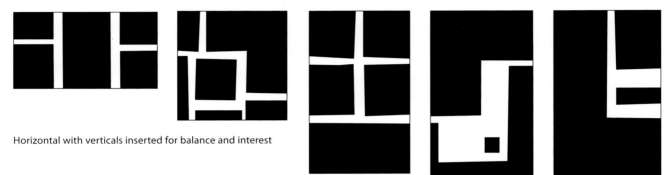

Horizontal with verticals inserted for balance and interest

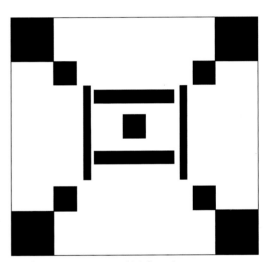

A radiating structure in which lines (or the main shapes of the objects) radiate out from the center or circle around a central point

The Affluent Drainpipe
by Elizabeth Barton
37″ × 55″

The main vertical axis is shifted slightly to the right to balance the weight of the window in the upper left.

Spring City **by Elizabeth Barton, 60″ × 60″**

Spring City has a circular structure that pulls the city together into a whole.

Distant Lights **by Elizabeth Barton, 38″ × 56″**

Grids are usually arranged in an allover design and provide a strong and well-balanced basic structure. They have been used for many a large building as well as lots of quilts. Grids can also be arranged in many different ways, which has made this basic structure very popular with quilt artists. Here, the different sections are arranged in a loose grid, which helps to pull them together.

Spires and Chimneys **by Elizabeth Barton, 26″ × 26″**

The triangular or pyramidal format of many early religious paintings was a very symmetrical basic structure and one that quilters use.

Usually the type of underlying structure would be obviously related to your subject, but you can choose something different. You could actually conceive of a series based on one topic and several different structures, for example, a series of quilts about water.

The Beach in Winter by Elizabeth Barton, 40″ × 26″

Horizontal structure

LightFall by Elizabeth Barton, 35″ × 76″

Vertical: Waterfall tumbling from the top to the bottom of the picture

Farne Islands by Elizabeth Barton, 60″ × 47″

Interlocking jigsaw pattern

I find that looking at possible structures helps me to come up with variations on my theme; it's a great way to generate design ideas and a lot more subtle than simply doing the same idea in different colors—though that too is a possibility.

POSITIVE AND NEGATIVE SPACE

Negative space is the area around the positive shape; sometimes these are referred to as *figure* (positive) versus *ground* (negative space). The painter Barnett Newman described an artist as a "choreographer of space." Every inch of your quilt should be thoughtfully considered; negative spaces should be examined as carefully as the positive spaces to ensure variety and contrast. If you are making a quilt with squares mounted on a background, examine the background shapes. Is the background quite mundane, uniform, and just sitting there, or could you tweak it a little to add some interest to the piece? Negative spaces do not need to be boring!

EXERCISE

Negative Space

1. Using construction paper in a dark shade, cut out some rectangles and squares and arrange them on a plain piece of white copy paper.

2. Look at the white negative space; make it boring. Then make it much more interesting. How can these shapes be arranged to make a walk around them a lot more interesting?

3. Then go a step further and begin to integrate the different parts of your positive spaces and negative spaces. Think about making one large intriguing white shape and one large fascinating black shape so the two shapes are interlocked in a way that sets your eyes dancing!

Pay attention to the negative as well as the positive! Take a look at your sketches for your quilt series, and focus only on the negative spaces. Do they add to the pieces? Can you improve them with just a little shifting around of the positive elements?

VISUAL PATHWAYS

Art books often discuss the importance of including visual pathways to lead the viewer's eyes around a work of art. These visual pathways include using a focal point (page 100) and "lines" leading to or away from the focal point. These can be real lines or curves, such as paths, edges of buildings, or drapery of some kind. Or they may be indicated by little highlights such as an opening at the base of the artwork, a break in a fence, or a trailing branch of a plant. This is a pathway the artist has made for you to follow, just as a landscape designer makes pathways for your feet. Frequently devices are used at the corners of the painting to turn your eye back into the piece so you don't wander off onto the next painting. Can you see these? Maybe they are cleverly disguised as a cloud or a swaying, bowed strand of grass.

Do Visual Pathways Really Work?

Visual pathways have been used for many years, and traditional textbooks state that they are vital in keeping the viewer engaged with your piece; however, recent research suggests that the way in which people examine an art piece is a lot more complicated than simply following a path. Scientists attached little sensors to volunteers' eyes so that they could actually see on a monitor where the people looked, how they got from point A to point B. The first thing that was evident was that eyes don't really need pathways. Viewers do not "take a walk" around a piece so much as flit from one interesting area to another. I don't think that actual pathways are really necessary but rather that the areas of importance to us, the areas that provide the keys to the whole piece, are very distinctive. The other areas are necessary as supports. Areas of high contrast, whether value, shape, color, or soft or hard edges, can be used to direct people's gaze to different areas in the quilt.

The Red Chimney by Elizabeth Barton, 54″ × 28″

Pump Court
by Elizabeth Barton
35″ × 48″

In this quilt, I've used a number of devices: perspective lines, leading back to draw you into the picture; the focal area is high contrast; and there's also a suggestion of a shadowy figure just disappearing into the light at the end of the alleyway.

Double Exposure: Spire by Elizabeth Barton, 48″ × 26″

In *Double Exposure: Spire*, I've used contrast between the two sides of the piece to attract the viewer to first one side and then the other.

The more you know about how people see things and how they process visual information, the more you can make your art have impact. For example, advertisers and web designers know from their research that people tend to look more readily at warmer colors than cool ones. Strong value contrasts are more likely to gain attention than subtle ones. Certain subjects are almost magnetically attractive, such as human beings, especially babies! Certain textures, patterns, intensities of color—all catch and hold attention. The most likely thing to catch our attention is movement, especially in a human being.

In classical paintings, the old masters would indicate movement by having the subjects of the paintings (especially the supporting cast) gaze directly at the important area. Nearly all the classical paintings of the crucifixion, for example, incorporate this feature: at the base of the cross, the suffering gaze upward, thus directing our gaze upward.

When looking at an image, we notice human beings first. Look at any painting, and you'll see how your eye is drawn to a figure, no matter how small. Painters often use the device of inserting small figures into the design. Does your series topic involve figures? You might be able to make an image more interesting with just the suggestion of a figure.

First we see people, and then we notice other living creatures. A small cat or a bird can liven up a piece, though this device has been used so often it can be a little trite! Be careful. After living beings, the next most likely things to attract are warm colors, strong value contrasts, and intriguing textures or patterns with intricate detail.

CHOOSING STRONG COLOR SCHEMES

Color nearly always has the first big impact on viewers and attracts them to a quilt. Good use of color is tremendously important, but it's difficult to manage well without knowledge and experience. So often people say, "Oh, I'm no good at color," as if there is nothing they can do about it. Color ability develops as the result of careful observation and practice, practice, practice. One of the most important errors when working from a specific inspiration is forgetting to really look. Somehow we've learned that grass and leaves are green, the sky is blue, tree trunks are brown, and so on. And yet if I really look out of my window, I see red and orange leaves, green-gray and black tree trunks, and a silvery sky. White clothes hanging on the line have blue and purple shadows, snow can have a pink or yellow cast to it, and the sky can be any color at all.

King's Square
by Elizabeth Barton
42˝ × 67˝

King's Square is an open square in the old town of York in England. For this quilt, I moved a few houses to make a better composition, and a green sky fit the color scheme well.

Be aware of all the color around you and of the effect of light, shade, and reflection. This will lead you to a much better sense of the marvelous variations and combinations that are available, more than any theoretical study or looking at little strips of colors printed onto cards. Also, visit an art museum and look at the way experienced painters use color. What strange combinations do they put together? How do they create mood and nuance with color? Why have they suddenly intensified the color in a specific section or added little flicks of a contrast color somewhere else? Think about the colors that painter John Blockley calls "dancing colors": violet, pink, white, and chartreuse.

Also, don't forget the neutrals. These are the means by which the dancing colors glow. How were the neutral colors arranged in those wonderful paintings and quilts that you've seen? And to what effect? I think it's especially important to look at the rich subtlety of less obvious colors: peat, bronze, charcoal, and pewter—the names alone evoke rich harmonies.

City of Mists
by Elizabeth Barton
40″ × 52″

City of Mists is based on several images of the flattening effects of mist—no depth and beautiful, soft, mysterious, varied grays.

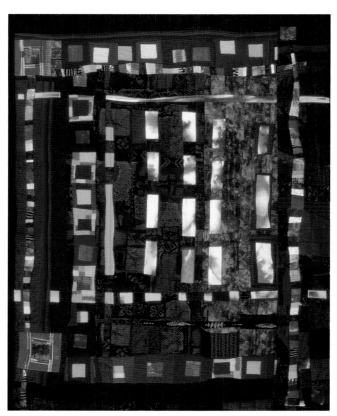

Scud
by Elizabeth Barton
42″ × 56″

Scud is based on my memory of lying on the floor underneath the large skylights looking up at the clouds scudding by.

HOW TO AVOID COMMON COLOR ERRORS

Too Many Colors

One of the most common color mistakes I see in art quilts is lack of discrimination. I call it the *"too muchness error"*—too much of this, too much of that, too much of everything. Always aim to have one main color that pulls everything together, creating unity. Of course you can have other colors, but one should predominate. If you think about your living room: you wouldn't paint the walls all different colors, have a multicolored carpet in different tones, and then put in chairs with even more colors, would you? It would feel very unsettled and inharmonious. The same thing is true in fashion: imagine an outfit where you had a green shirt, red trousers, blue socks, white shoes, a yellow cardigan, and a purple scarf!! But I have seen so many quilts that are green

and red and blue and white and yellow and fuchsia and purple and brown and, oh, let's add a dash of black too—why not?

And then there are those who exercise too much restraint. They might choose lavender and yellow for their quilt, and make every yellow piece the exact same yellow, and every lavender shape the same fabric. No! Too flat. Too boring. Use nature as an example: Look at a bunch of purple petunias. Every shade of purple, from almost pink to violet, and every gradation of value will be represented. To make your art quilt rich in color, vary the values, shades, tones, and temperatures of the dominant color.

Too Many Colors in the Same Value

The term *value* refers to the degree of lightness or darkness of a color. All colors can vary from very pale, through midtones, to very dark, though some will have a greater range. Blue can go from the merest, palest tint of an ice blue through to a deep, dark midnight blue, whereas yellow has a much more limited range.

An art quilt that has a good range of values (pale, medium, and dark color) will have both strength and clarity. If all the colors are midtones, the work can look rather muddy. Take a photo of your quilt and photocopy it in black and white to check. Or, if you have a photo-editing program on your computer (page 67), desaturate the image (remove color while retaining the values) to see the piece in shades of gray. If the design and structure of the image disappear when you do this, then your value choices are at fault. Even very saturated, intense colors can completely disappear if they are the same value as the colors around them.

Whenever you're uncertain about your choice of fabrics, take a photo of them arranged together and desaturate. Remember, identical values lead to mud! Try to have a variety, but as with hue, choose one to be dominant.

Color ranges of yellow and blue

Too Many Colors with the Same Degree of Saturation/Intensity

The terms *saturation* and *intensity* refer to the pureness of the color. To see this, find a very rich green fabric in your stash. Now look for a very grayed green. Repeat this with two other colors. Can you see the difference between the saturated colors and the grayed ones? Take your favorite color (that's the one you have the most of), cut out squares from all the different fabrics, and make an intensity or saturation scale. The most intense colors are in the middle of the value range. They are not pale (pale colors are generally lower in intensity), nor are they very dark (dark colors are often a mix of colors and not very pure). Making a scale like this will help you to become much more aware of variations in saturation.

The light values are on the left, the medium values in the middle, and the dark values on the right. The most saturated colors (the most intense) are in the middle of the value range, as can be seen in the white/gray/black version.

Three intensities (saturations) of red hand-dyed fabric

A quilt that is made with nothing but very saturated colors looks like an advertisement for M&Ms or similar candied confection. On the other hand, if you have no intense colors, it can look very flat and dull. As with spices, use intensity wisely: A little bit is good, but too much and you have ruined the flavor of the piece. Moderation rules.

Too Many Colors in the Same Temperature

Colors can be considered *warm* or *cool*: Yellows, oranges, and reds are warm; blues and greens are cool. However, it is important to remember that temperature is *largely relative*. Instead of considering one particular color warm or cool, consider colors in pairs; in each pair, one is warmer and one is cooler.

Which is the cooler color? The one that is nearer to the cooler section of the color wheel (the blue and green section). The warmer color is the one that is nearer to the warmer section.

Take a pair of reds: say, scarlet and fuchsia. Look at them side by side. Scarlet is warmer than fuchsia. It is nearer to orange on the wheel; fuchsia is nearer to purple.

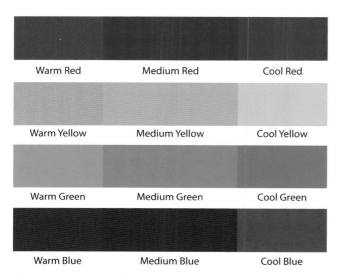

Warm, medium, and cool colors

It helps to clarify and unify a work of art if *one color temperature is dominant*; the quilt colors should be overall cool or overall warm. Choose which according to your main theme. However, don't have every single piece of fabric the same temperature. If it's all warm or all cool, the piece will not be as strong. A little dash of the other temperature (warm if it's a cool piece and vice versa) will actually enhance the overall effect.

Color Temperature

If you feel you are still unsure about color temperature, make some more examples.

1. Pull out 2 pieces of yellow, 2 of blue, 2 of green, and 2 of purple fabric. Can you see which yellow is warmer? The one that is more buttery. The cool yellow is more lemony—there are a few green tones in it. Some blues are quite icy like a glacier with underlying green tones. Others are warm like a cornflower or a summer sky with very faint pink hints in them.

2. If you have access to any watercolors, try this: Paint a long stripe of the bluest blue you can. Cobalt blue is generally accepted to be the most neutral in temperature. While the paint is wet, add a tiny drop of green to one end and a tiny drop of very diluted red (pink) to the other end—not enough to change the hue, but just to shift the temperature slightly. Can you see the difference? Now try it with several other colors so that the concept is clear.

SIMULTANEOUS CONTRAST

Color varies on four different dimensions: hue, value, intensity (or saturation), and temperature. Each one of these is enhanced when you add a little dash of the opposite into your quilt, or your home, or your outfit. A winter scene with ice and snow, all blue and white and cold, is enhanced by a tiny touch of orange or red: a holly berry, a skier's jacket, or a red cardinal. A desert scene in yellow and orange sand looks richer with a hint of violet in the shadows. This is called *simultaneous contrast*: putting a small piece of the opposite hue, value, intensity, or temperature next to a color will enhance that color.

USING VALUE PATTERNS

The terms *value pattern*, *chiaroscuro*, and *notan* all describe the light–dark pattern that underlies every good composition. Sometimes called *tone* in older textbooks, *value* refers to how light or dark anything is.

Chiaroscuro

A word of Italian origin that translates as light-dark, *chiaroscuro* is generally used to describe work with strong light–dark contrast. Sometimes it refers to the way volume can be indicated by increasing amounts of shading. In an art quilt you can do this either with the density of your stitches or by layering transparent fabrics.

Photo by Karen J. Hamrick

The Cove | In *The Cove* I emphasized the darks and lights by
by Elizabeth Barton | minimizing color and by contrasting the stitching:
31″ × 39″ | dark over light, light over dark.

Notan

A word of Japanese origin meaning dark-light, *notan* actually refers to the interaction between positive (light) elements and negative (dark) ones. This is clearly expressed visually by the very old yin-yang symbol of dual forces in unity.

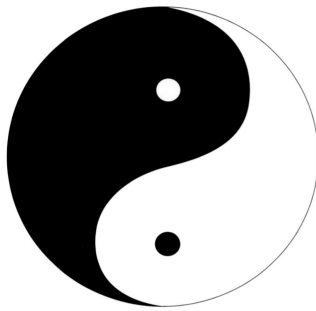

Yin-yang symbol

Each of the above terms has a slightly different meaning, but they all emphasize not only the importance of having a dark–light underlying pattern but also the absolute necessity of it in work that expresses the human condition. The power of the contrast between light and dark, between positive and negative, is vital in any kind of design, philosophy, law, and even storytelling.

How to See and Use Value Patterns

If you close your eyes halfway when you look at a scene or image, you reduce the light and your brain will then read the value pattern rather than the color pattern. Try this when looking at a great painting, and a strong pattern of dark and light shapes will be clearly evident. An interesting and well-balanced value pattern helps to pull your piece together. When you look at any artwork, your eye goes immediately to the strongest contrast between dark and light in a piece. Which of the squares below did you notice first?

Notice the area with the strongest contrast in value.

Using this type of value contrast helps you establish your focal areas. We are actually hardwired to pay attention to high contrasts. Babies focus on faces because it literally helps in their survival: They look for the contrast of hairline, forehead, and eyebrows. A parent cares for a child that searches for his/her face and clearly reacts positively to it. This is why babies pay more attention to objects with a high contrast of values (such as black and white) than to those with very soft pastel coloring. So if you are making a baby quilt, black and white is the way to go if you want the baby to like it (even if it doesn't match the colors of the baby's room).

Using negative space (page 78) well is also part of using value effectively. Take an art quilt design you are unsure of and reduce it to just black and white (repeatedly photocopying your photocopy will do this). If the final result looks boring, unbalanced, or chaotic, cut out the dark shapes and rearrange them on a new sheet of white paper. After rearranging, check it again for interest and for balance. Balance that is very symmetrical is very static—though decorative, it doesn't hold anyone's interest for as long. People are attracted by differences and oddities, though of course you always want the shapes to relate to one another, and it's even better if their interactions are relevant to the content of your piece. Imbalance or tension (a little, not too much) increases interest without leading us into confusion and chaos.

Photo by Karen J. Hamrick

Separate and Together
by Elizabeth Barton
33″ × 59″

In *Separate and Together* and several other quilts from my black-and-white series (pages 4–6, 75, and 106), I've used an asymmetrical balance to make them more interesting.

APPLYING LANDSCAPE PAINTING COMPOSITION GUIDELINES TO ART QUILTS

As art quilters we can learn so much from reading about painting. *Carlson's Guide to Landscape Painting,* by John F. Carlson, is one of the best books ever written on the topic. He constantly emphasizes the importance of keeping the main structure of the piece simple. A simple, clear underlying structure (as with a building or town plan) unifies your quilt. It also strengthens its appearance from a distance, so as the visitors enter a gallery or exhibit, your quilt will be one that stands out. A strong composition will consist of four or five large shapes of varying value with only *necessary* detail added to them. A composition is simply an arrangement of elements (in two-dimensional art: line, shape, value, color, and texture). It helps to think of the objects in your design in abstract terms: not a house but rather a square or a rectangle; not a tree but a circle with a line (or rectangle) emerging from the bottom. This will make arranging them in the *picture plane* (defined by the edges of the quilt) much easier. The task is to arrange the major elements in a way that is pleasing, communicative, challenging, unforgettable, and, in particular, unfussy. Carlson wrote: "There probably never was a picture that was poor because it lacked detail or subject matter; rather the opposite. Bad paintings are usually so overloaded with useless detail that the essentials are obliterated."

Another important observation from Carlson is, "We must have design even at the expense of truth." In other words, don't focus unduly on the colors or textures or arrangement of shapes you have in your photograph; if something doesn't make a good design, change it. Use not what is real but what is *right* for your quilt, as Rembrandt did with his lighting patterns. The important thing is that the elements are organized in the most interesting and truth-revealing way— which is not necessarily how they appear in real life.

Think about design as a way to reveal the beauty of common things and to do more than merely render the shapes of the objects you see. Begin with close observation, a keen consideration of the main shapes, values, and colors. Make notes, sketches, and so on. But when you begin to work on the piece, you must add your thoughts and feelings. To say something vital and important about, say, the beauty of a dumpster with its rusty stains and scratches, you must add your full and loving appreciation of it to the image. It's easier to do this if you're not too hung up on making a literal copy. This is why I think it is better to work from a small sketch rather than a full-size cartoon. With the small sketch you can get the main shapes and values, and then as you build the quilt, you add all those nuances that are coming from your imagination and your heart. Memory exaggerates the essentials, and the trifles become blurred. Carlson says that copying what is exactly there "dulls the initial expressive shock." Memory filters out the nonessential. It is the artist's task to nudge the viewer into seeing these hidden beauties. Consider an arrangement of something as prosaic as empty bottles.

Photo by Karen J. Hamrick

Colliery by Elizabeth Barton, 18″ × 24″

The old winding wheels of the collieries (coal mines and the related buildings) were rarely seen this highlighted against a dark sky, but were often jumbled in with other shapes. In this quilt, I've focused only on the key shapes, while in real life there were a lot more fiddly bits. The confusion of extra shapes would have made the design much weaker.

Who ever looked twice at a group of old bottles before Giorgio Morandi lovingly painted their nuances of color and form? Dominie Nash uses a similar theme.

Monet revealed the evanescence of light on haystacks. Photographs of the actual scenes that Cézanne or Van Gogh painted appear at first glance to be very ordinary and prosaic until the artists pointed out their subtle beauty. The truth is, you don't have to go to Provence or Venice to find wondrous ideas; they are right outside your front door.

Photo by Mark Gulezian/QuickSilver Photographers

EXERCISE

Simplification

Carlson continually emphasized the importance of being simple, focused, and direct. Simplification exercises are very helpful.

1. Using any photograph, for example, a market scene, make a straightforward sketch, trying to be as accurate as you can.

2. Make several more sketches, emphasizing only a single specific idea, such as the pattern of the cloths covering the booths, the people, the produce, or the interweaving verticals. In a landscape you could make a sketch focusing on the trees, the sky, a house or cottage, the flowers, or the people in the landscape.

3. Pin up your sketches (I hope you have five or six of them) on the wall and you will see that when you focus in on making just *one* thing the main area of interest, the piece as a whole becomes stronger.

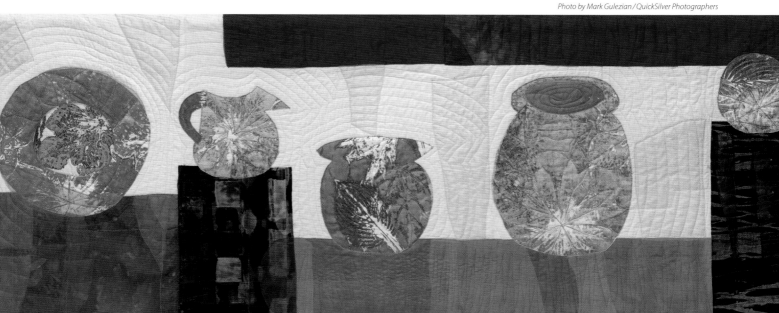

Still Life #41 **by Dominie Nash, 70″ × 26″**

Storm Dance
by Elizabeth Barton
18″ × 23″

The theme for this quilt is the trees dancing in stormy winds. The outline of the house against the dark night emphasizes the Halloween feel, but I've omitted much more than I've included.

CREATING THE ILLUSION OF DEPTH

Achieving a sense of depth in a quilt is one of the most frequently requested discussions in my workshops. People also worry about perspective and think that getting the perspective right is the best way to indicate depth. Perspective, however, is really more important in architectural, technical, or very classical drawing than in designing for an art piece. If you look at paintings today, you'll rarely see perspective lines used to any great extent. In fact, a recent study of several of even Vermeer's paintings revealed significant problems with perspective. So I think it's a lot less important than people consider. Furthermore, being too obsessive about perspective can tighten up the work. So if you want to convey a sense of depth, use the techniques the painters use (as follows), rather than those employed by architects.

Color and Value

Ferrybridge
by Elizabeth Barton
60″ × 58″

The color and value become softer the farther back the objects are. Color and value changes are probably the most important devices for creating depth. A good way to create the illusion of recession within the picture space is through a very dark yet clear foreground leading to a light atmospheric background.

Overlapping

Echoes in the Memory **by Elizabeth Barton, 60″ × 65″**

The city retreats into the distance as one building overlaps another.

Size Change

Placement

The Red Gate **by Elizabeth Barton, 39″ × 63″**

You see that the buildings at the top of the steps are farther away, in part because they are higher up on the quilt.

Age Cannot Wither
by Elizabeth Barton
62″ × 84″

In *Age Cannot Wither* the buildings become smaller as they are farther away from the viewer.

Foreground, Middle Ground, Background

The traditional way of incorporating a sense of depth into an artwork is to have a foreground, middle ground, and background. As you build your quilt on the design wall, begin with the farthest point back in the landscape and gradually add fabric pieces on top. As you come forward, use fabrics that have more contrast in value, more details, and more saturated colors to give your quilt depth.

Linear Perspective

Perspective can be a useful tool in indicating depth, but I suggest you keep it simple. For example, a fence line where the posts gradually become smaller and closer together suggests receding space.

The strange thing about perspective is that it assumes you are standing completely still in one spot with one eye closed, like a camera! Usually, however, we are making artworks about our own experience and not about being a camera. We have two eyes, each seeing a slightly different version of the scene, and moreover, we move about a lot. Try this experiment: Arrange a few items on a tabletop, crouch down so that you're at eye level with them, and then look first with one eye and then the other. You will see everything shift slightly to one side—all the relationships between the objects change. And that's just one second of your experience. We are constantly moving, and our brains are being flooded with different impressions; there's never just one fixed angle of perspective. The only way to get a single fixed view is in fact through a camera, but problems can arise in working with a camera too, as we'll discuss in the next paragraph.

Looking Back
by Elizabeth Barton
46˝ × 60˝

PROBLEMS WITH WORKING FROM PHOTOGRAPHS

Throughout this book, I've talked about using photographs as inspiration. As with fire, photographs are a great servant but a bad master. In some situations photographs are really helpful, such as with moving objects or people, but there are pitfalls also. Artists have worked from photographs for a very long time. David Hockney demonstrated that even back in Renaissance times, artists knew about pinhole cameras, and it is quite possible that they used them. It is fascinating to look at the way a great painter will interpret a photograph of a fairly boring scene and make an exciting painting from it. If you can find books in the library that show a photograph and the resulting painting, they are well worth studying. What did the artist do to improve the photograph? Are there any ideas there that you can use? Working from photographs is perfectly legitimate, and with knowledge and forethought you can avoid the following problems.

PROBLEM 1 · *Limited to the concrete*

One of the main difficulties with photography is that the camera's eye is indiscriminate and dispassionate, but good art should always include the artist. The artist's feelings, reactions, and impressions bring life to a work of art. Take several photographs of the inspirational landscape or object so that you're not locked into just one view or aspect, and jot down the reasons you were drawn to the scene, such as follows:

- I love the effect of the mist flattening all the shapes— so magical.
- Those are wonderful shadows dancing on the wall.
- The juxtaposition of turquoise, black, and orange on the torn posters on the old wall is so vibrant.

When you get home and look at the photo, those colors almost certainly will not look as vibrant as you remembered. Don't delete the photo, thinking that it's not very interesting; instead, make art based on the photo *plus* your notes *plus* your memory of your delight.

Three Views by **Elizabeth Barton** 75″ × 25″

These pieces are views of my house, each focusing on specific features that come to mind as I think of the house: pointed roof with blue skies, front door, and foliage. None of them are literal, just what is important to me.

PROBLEM 2 *Too inclusive*

The camera makes no decisions as to what to include and what to leave out. All the details are present, whether they add or detract. In fact, the focal area of interest may be practically engulfed by extraneous detail. When we look at something, we focus on the one thing that interests us, it looks brighter and clearer because of our focus, and the surroundings are blurry and duller. As you look at your photos, ask yourself, What is the most important thing here, and what can I omit? Gaze at the photo closely for a minute, put it aside, and then quickly draw the features that stick in your mind. This helps you to see what is important to you and, even more useful, what is not. Keep only those secondary details that are necessary for balance or contrast. If you find you are being seduced by some random detail in the image, make a note of it—or another quilt!

PROBLEM 3 *Absence*

The photo shows only what is there, but sometimes things need to be added. In a landscape, you may need to add a third tree if two are standing like stiff sentinels not looking in the least bit natural. A wall may be too blank and boring and need to be broken up a little. A flower arrangement might have an awkward gap. An abstract pattern of dots and squares might have a large area that doesn't connect to other areas. Don't feel that you can't add something to your design just because it wasn't in the photograph. The artist is always free to subtract and to add. Perhaps adding a shape might improve the balance, or changing a bird from brown to red might add some sparkle. A shape might need to have some lumps removed because they look odd and detract from the overall unity.

PROBLEM 4 *Awkward juxtapositions*

Sometime objects line up in a rather peculiar way or perhaps too rigid a way. Telephone poles can sprout from people's heads; feet can completely disappear into shadow; buildings can line up in odd ways.

PROBLEM 5 *Distorted values*

Real-life shadows are subtle and rich, full of nuance. But photographed shadows are often just large black blobs. The camera tends to overemphasize dark values and push them toward black; light values might be totally bleached out. So always make note of the colors you actually see in the darker and lighter areas when you take the photo so you can be sure to include them in your design.

PROBLEM 6 *Color that is too literal*

Furthermore, don't let yourself be distracted by the actual color of an object in a photograph. Color is really quite arbitrary and can, and often should, be changed to improve a composition. The focal area will stand out if it has the greatest contrast in color (whether the contrast is in hue, value, intensity, or temperature). If that is not evident in your photograph, too bad; but you, the artist, can make sure it is there in your actual piece. Alternatively, the opposite can happen: Some object, say a small child in a red raincoat, may be right at the edge of the image, and that spot of bright red will draw the eye away from the composition as a whole. Working from a black-and-white photocopy of your photograph will help you to follow value rather than color in your composition. Then when you have the value studies worked out, you can decide where to put the spots of bright color based on your composition rather than your photo.

PROBLEM 7 *Too realistic*

When photography was first invented, classical painters were both intrigued and intimidated by the artistry and truthfulness of the early photographs. The impressionists, however, decided that since photography could re-create reality, painting (and other two-dimensional arts) were now freed from needing to do this. Instead they could think about creating something that could not be achieved by a photograph. It makes sense—a painting, or a quilt, should not try to do what a photograph could do better. The artist must add something more. Otherwise, why not simply take a photograph of a scene instead of making a quilt? And so, in some ways the camera frees the artist.

The original photo

Moor Farm
by Elizabeth Barton
38″ × 24″

In *Moor Farm*, I used only those elements from the photo that really intrigued me: the contrast of the texture of the buildings with the vegetation around. I left no black shadows, made the colors richer, and simplified the shapes.

THE DYNAMIC QUILT

Questions I'm often asked in workshops are, "How do I make my quilt more exciting?" and, "How do you put tension or edge into a quilt?"

Tension, Unpredictability, and Contrast

In art, unpredictability is extremely desirable. Matisse wrote: "Ready-made images are for the eye what prejudices are for the mind." That is, they limit you. Going back to basics helps you to figure out how to be unpredictable. A composition is an arrangement of shapes and lines of varying values and colors. While it's important that the arrangement should be unified and harmonious, if everything fits together too well, you lose dynamism. A quilt can then become very boring and conventional. Sometimes a nice quiet day at the office is good, but too many of them and you start to yawn and fall asleep on the job. Contrast, or variety, is crucial for keeping us awake. A little tension or edginess makes for a lot of interest. Don't have every shape completely predictable or all the colors pastel and sweet. Avoid too much beige. Even a quiet life needs a bit of sparkle here and there. It's important to have some contrast, a little edginess.

Asymmetry

Symmetry and asymmetry work together to create dynamic quilts. A piece that has symmetry without the tension of asymmetry is predictable and boring, whereas a design that feels balanced yet looks asymmetrically off-balance is exciting. A strong design should keep you wondering. It used to be thought that homeostasis (everything in balance, everything just right) was good for human beings; now we know that we are more alert, more interested, and more active if we're slightly out of balance. And the same holds true in art. Some symmetry is good—for it's difficult to look at a piece where a heavy weight on one side is pulling it down—but perfect symmetry can get quite tedious. Asymmetry is actually not so much a lack of symmetry as it is a balance achieved by means other than identical placement of identical objects.

Repetition with Change

Repeating any element creates rhythm and movement, which make a work of art much more exciting. When a shape, line, or color is repeated, the first thing we notice is that those elements belong together. If you saw a tree with every leaf a different shape and color, you would think it was strange and artificial, a weird mix. But, if the opposite were true and the tree had every single leaf the exact same size, color, and shape, that too would be problematic, though for a different reason—it would look artificial and dead. Nature is one of art's best teachers: leaves on a tree obviously belong together, the shapes are very similar, as are the colors, but the little shifts in value and tone make it real and exciting.

Most compositions (whether art, music, dance, poetry, or prose) involve a basic structure of repeated elements. Variety (contrast, tension) is the counterweight of repetition. A piece of music often begins with a series of the same note, but notice how, although the note is the same, the emphasis, or the length, or the color of the note varies. And that's what makes that phrase true: If you made a quilt about a fence and every board were perfect, it would be an architectural drawing. If you had a knothole here, a slight lean there, and a gap somewhere else, it would begin to be a lot more interesting. So think about this when your design involves a row of trees, or houses, or even amorphous blobs.

Stanley by Elizabeth Barton, 44″ × 60″

Guildhall by Elizabeth Barton, 44″ × 60″

Quilts about buildings where every window is identical look so static; every window a little different is so much more exciting. This is why Anna Williams's way of free-cutting the fabric, discovered by Nancy Crow and taught to a whole generation of quilt-makers, was so effective and revolutionary. Being a little looser leads to rhythms and variations that bring the work to life.

Inspired Use of Negative Space

Not only is the actual object important in repetition and rhythm, but the space between the notes or objects (the negative space) is vital too. The repeated interrelationship of sequences and the rhythms between any of the design elements strongly support unity with variety. Rhythmical sequences such as rough-smooth-rough-smooth or straight-curved-straight-curved create unity and harmony, but slight differences in the intervals will syncopate the rhythms and maximize our interest.

Many artists use repetitions with variation to make their work more dynamic. Frank Webb (learning from Cézanne) likes alternations of cool and warm, which he feels adds excitement. An artist is a "choreographer of space" (Barnett Newman); every inch of the piece should be consciously considered to achieve the most interest. Look carefully at the negative spaces as well as the positive shapes to make sure there is variety and contrast.

If you are making a quilt with squares mounted on a background, look at the background grid. Is it totally uniform? Could you tweak it a little to gain some interest? Some uncertainty? Your piece will be stronger for it. Any comedian will tell you that timing is everything—consider carefully the space between the elements (the pause before the punch line) before you bring in your punch line of the focal point!

Equally sized positive objects, equally sized negative spaces

Variably sized positive objects, equally sized negative spaces

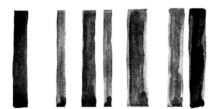

Variably sized positive *and* negative spaces

Differences in intervals create interest.

Battersea by Elizabeth Barton, 18″ × 24″

Notice that every chimney is different.

Photo by Karen J. Hamrick

Movement

Human beings are wired to pay attention to moving objects. An indication of movement brings vitality to any artwork. The effect of movement in two-dimensional art can be created by a number of different manipulations of any of the elements. Diagonal lines suggest the forward movement of the human body; gradations of color or value indicate advancing or retreating shapes. Lines can soften and disappear; cloud shapes can look solid and momentous, or ragged and strewn across the sky. Research the Internet or visit a gallery and look for the ways in which other artists have indicated movement. For example, one could suggest the wind with scudding sails and blowing flags, all the flags aloft, rippled and stretched out in the same direction.

If you have movement, however, you should also have the balancing effect of countermovement. The best pieces demonstrate a balance of movement and countermovement, of weight and counterweight. The signs of movement, whether they are scudding sails or blowing flags, should be countered by an opposite force. In most simplistic terms, if the wind is pushing the sailboats to the left, then you might counter this with anchored boats at the quayside with their prows pointing to the right. If your piece has diagonals all pointing one way, it upsets the balance and also is less interesting.

Forcefield 2 by Elizabeth Barton, 48″ × 27″

In an abstract piece devoted to pure pattern, the same principle holds true: If all the shapes point in one direction, it is less dynamic than if one or two are directed in the opposite way.

Look at Degas's paintings of dancers. His pictures are masterworks of dynamic design and demonstrate the great importance of balance and rhythm. See how he creates movement and a visual path for the eye along the arms of the dancers, which leads to the next point, further enhanced by contrasting the very light values against a dark background. Don't think that Degas was lucky enough to just capture this scene in reality. The paintings are as carefully choreographed as the dancers themselves.

Countermovement can also be indicated by gradation, which suggests a diminution in intensity of the implied movement toward the edges of the piece. Gradually reducing value, color, or saturation slows the movement. Classical painters used these devices constantly. As an art quilt designer, I suggest you keep these ideas in mind when evaluating your work. I'm not suggesting, however, that you try to worry about all these points from the outset. The first task is just to generate ideas. Later, when you come to decide which sketches to use for your series, consider how you might make these designs more dynamic.

Photo by Karen J. Hamrick

Rooflines by Elizabeth Barton, 49″ × 24″

In this quilt I deliberately altered the angle of some of the roofs to counter the strong directionality of the diagonals. I also made sure there were plenty of verticals to counter the strong horizontal movement of the roof lines and tiles.

---

tip *Capturing Attention*

If you want to capture viewers' attention, you need to have something that makes them want to look twice— something intriguing that makes them stop and look and look; some little quirk, a variation, a lack of balance, some tension. Consider each element: Could more subtle variety be included? Should it be gradual or sudden? Is there movement? And countermovement? Above all: Don't be predictable!

Focal Areas and Emphasis

You often hear people talking about a focal point in an artwork and probably wonder if you need to have one, and if so, why. A focal point grabs attention, and when that happens, a viewer will be more likely to stay with a piece for a while. The emphasized area draws people in, and after they've looked at the most important area, they begin to look at the less dramatic sections too. A work can of course have more than one focal point, but the others should be secondary. You want only one lead tenor in the opera. Size is unimportant; it's impact that counts. The focal point can be quite small or as much as 25 percent of the quilt. You can emphasize your focal area by contrast (of any of the elements), isolation, and placement.

Coppergate **by Elizabeth Barton, 38″ × 63″**

Note how value contrast and color saturation decrease away from the central focal area.

Photo by Karen J. Hamrick

Backstreet **by Elizabeth Barton, 36″ × 51″**

The orange element in the center is both a brighter color than the rest of the shapes and a much less regular shape, which make it stand out.

Chimneys **by Elizabeth Barton, 24″ × 24″**

Botallack Mine **by Elizabeth Barton, 28″ × 39″**

Photo by Karen J. Hamrick

In both of these quilts, the lone chimney isolated in the sky or against a contrasting background first draws attention.

Photo by Karen J. Hamrick

Ambivalence **by Elizabeth Barton, 48″ × 72″**

In *Ambivalence* the lines lead upward toward the top area of the quilt, emphasizing the height of these towering elevators.

Make a point as you look at printed or painted images to see if you can figure out how the artist or designer has drawn your attention to the focus of the piece. Remember that the focal point should relate to the rest of the piece. If it has no relation to it at all, you will definitely spot it, but it will be awkward and disjointed.

tip *Must You Have a Focal Point?*

Focal points are not necessary; they are merely a device to draw the viewer's attention to the meaning of the piece. It's quite possible to make a painting or an art quilt without one. Think of Andy Warhol's soup can paintings: rows upon rows of cans of soup stacked up, each one identical. Why might that be? Seeing such conspicuous repetition leads us to think about it, and in trying to puzzle it out, he has caught our attention. Many beautiful traditional quilts do not have focal areas but gain our attention because of their overall balance, simplicity, and calmness. Or, as in the quilt below, activity everywhere on a busy building site is indicated.

Photo by Karen J. Hamrick

Steel Reflections **by Elizabeth Barton, 24″ × 18″**

GESTALT DESIGN PRINCIPLES

The gestalt phenomenon is also frequently used to attract and focus the viewer. *Gestalt* is a word of German origin meaning "form" or "configuration." Gestalt theories of visual perception help us to understand how the eye and brain process visual information to create simple, symmetrical, and predictable patterns. As an exercise, quickly draw an O, but don't quite complete the circle, leave a small opening. Now ask the next person you see what letter you have written or what shape you have drawn. Even though your O is incomplete, most people will visually complete the shape and say you have drawn a circle or written the letter O. This is what gestalt theory predicts. Lots of further examples of this are on the Internet.

This happens, it is thought, because closed shapes are more visually stable than unclosed shapes. If enough significant information is available, the mind will close gaps and complete unfinished forms. This is why it is actually better *not* to dot all your i's and cross all your t's in your quilt design—let the viewer complete those images. An example that you see very frequently is that of windows; you do not need to put in all four sides of the frame, then all of the inner frame, then all the divisions, and so on. Just indicate the frame as succinctly as you can, and the viewer's brain will take care of the rest. Indicating things more subtly will help to keep viewers interested in your piece. If too much is done for us, we'll move right on to the next quilt hanging in the show!

Cape Cornwall
by Elizabeth Barton
40″ × 49″

In this quilt, I've often just suggested a window, door, or chimney rather than completely spelling out every detail.

Gestalt theory also states that when a person starts to look in a particular direction, his eyes will continue in that direction until they are diverted by something significant. How can we use this scientific knowledge in our art quilt designs? We can direct the viewer to the main areas of the quilt that we want to emphasize by the use of lines and arrows: the direction of the gaze of any people portrayed in the piece, the sequencing of objects in the scene, perspective lines, and implied motion. Obviously you don't want to overuse this, but if you have a quilt where you feel that the focal area is likely to be overlooked because it is very subtle, then try it. It's another tool in your quilting repertoire.

Assembly
by Elizabeth Barton
39˝ × 37′

In *Assembly* I used several devices to engage viewers and keep their eyes moving: incomplete shapes, value pathways, and contrast.

SHIBUI: POWER OF THE MARK OF THE HAND

Shibui (or *shibusa*) is the Japanese word that describes how a work of art (whatever the medium) reveals the hand of the maker. In Japanese culture this quality is much revered and sought after. This is a very different concept from Western standards of excellence—as in quilt show judges who define excellent quilting as that which does *not* show the hand of the maker! *Shibui* celebrates a natural form and texture (the beauty of the fiber and the stitch itself); it also suggests a quietness, a simple flow, and thus an elegance. To me, a quilt that appears to be obsessively perfect and machine made is neither fascinating nor inspiring, for it is the twists and turns of nature that bring a piece to life.

Shibui refers to an irregularity of form; an openness to nature, roughness of texture, and the natural world. It is a concept appropriate to any medium. While perfection may be the goal in making a car, in art, perfection is boring, trite, mechanistic, materialistic, and without soul. *Shibui* shows the

human being at work. It celebrates naturalness, the hand of the maker, the artist's gestures, and also the accidental occurrences of the process of making art. A friend of mine, a painter, considers that a drip that occurs in the painting as she carries her loaded brush across to be part of the painting. While this concept is not a Western one, many Western artists are beginning to appreciate the subtlety, validity, and truth of this approach.

So, do not fret if you run out of a certain fabric; add in a little bit more of something slightly different. The truth about life is that we *do* run out of things. Do not worry if your free-motion machine stitching is not all mathematically the same length. When we go round a curve, we do tend to slow down; it is good that the stitch length shows that. Once you have the main structure well balanced, you can allow yourself some freedom with the details. Let the work of your hands show in your piece.

CHAPTER 5

SHOWING YOUR WORK

You're working on your series, and you want to push your work to a level high enough to get into prestigious shows or even a solo show. How can you make that more likely? The following are some of the qualities I've noted from seeing many shows and talking to jurors.

QUALITIES TO STRIVE FOR

Originality

Jurors place tremendous importance on originality. We are all attracted by something new and are bored by repetitive or derivative works. A good art quilt should reveal a fresh and a personal vision. There should be some evidence of the artist herself and her humanity, style of working, and way of looking at the world. It doesn't matter if the work is abstract or representational—you can have fresh or stale work of either kind.

Attention Getting

Well-designed work is attention getting—it has both depth and staying power. You catch the viewers' eye from across the room and draw them in. As they get closer and closer, they discover more and more delights. If they go on to the next room in the gallery, they find themselves wanting to come back for a further look. There are, of course, a number of ways of getting attention. One of the most used is *tension* (page 96): the viewer is intrigued by unexpected unpredictability, an unsuspected variety or imbalance. This is why we were all so fascinated by the Gees Bend quilts—they broke the rules, the lines just didn't quite match up, and the pattern was left slightly incomplete or changed in unusual ways.

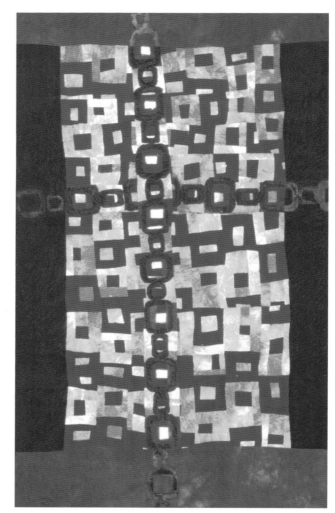

Chain Cross **by Elizabeth Barton, 37″ × 60″**

In *Chain Cross* the lines and squares don't match up exactly, which makes it much more interesting.

Strong Composition

Composition is defined as the arrangement of lines, shapes, values, colors, and textures; and that's exactly the task ahead of you when you start to arrange fabric on your design wall—nothing more, nothing less. What you're pinning onto the wall isn't a house but a square or a rectangle, not a tree or a head but a circle or oval. Thinking abstractly rather than representationally will help you to see how strong your design is. Think in terms of arranging overlapping squares on a background rather than houses in a landscape, triangles in space rather than yachts on the sea or trees in a field, interlocking lines rather than tree branches, triangles on a circle rather than the cat's face. Don't forget the basic design guidelines of harmony or unity, variety, rhythms and movement, balance and proportion, and economy. These guidelines have been derived by teachers of art over the centuries by looking at masterworks and analyzing just why those works are so successful.

In a work of art all the elements need to work together. A piece should be unified in and of itself. It should be cohesive, integrated, and possess an internal logic. Furthermore, the whole should be greater than the sum of the parts. It should also have some variety; otherwise you run the risk of being boring—as Shakespeare noted about Cleopatra:

> "Age cannot wither her, nor custom stale
> Her infinite variety; other women cloy."

We do not want our quilts to be either stale or cloying.

In strong compositions, the use of color and value (pages 80–87) is thoughtful and supports the basic meaning of the piece. Negative spaces (page 78) should be interesting and well used. It's better if the piece is not too busy, unless that is the central theme of the work. Balance, scale, and proportion are all important, and your quilts will be better if you keep these properties in mind.

Of course any "rules" of art can be broken when there is a particular reason to do so. For example, you might want to upset the balance and make a design quite top-heavy if your theme is "the weight of the world."

Every chimney is a bit different. All art forms have a basic structure of repeated elements, and all also include some variety or contrast within the repetition to prevent them from being boring or tedious.

Photo by Karen J. Hamrick

O Fortuna **by Elizabeth Barton, 27˝ × 41˝**

In *O Fortuna* shapes are repeated, but never identically. The weight of the large head gear wheel is supported by the structure beneath. Heavy shapes are under tension, tethered by delicate lines.

Photo by Karen J. Hamrick

Brighter at the Top **by Elizabeth Barton, 44˝ × 30˝**

Photo upon which *Sliding Edge* was based

Photo by Karen J. Hamrick

Sliding Edge by Elizabeth Barton 32″ × 54″

When I made *Sliding Edge*, my aim was to avoid being too literal and too detailed. I wanted to contrast soft with hard, undulating lines with straight ones, and color versus black and white. Remember, when working from a photograph, don't blindly copy every detail, but enrich the image, adding your feelings, hopes, and dreams.

Communication of Intention

Overall, a work of art is best assessed on the merit of the ideas it communicates to the observer and the interaction between the viewer and the work. Looking at your quilt top on the design wall, ask yourself if the design communicates your intention in making the piece. Does your message come across? Is the message trite and banal, or have you managed to communicate something very personal that comes from your own experience, your mind, your heart? Was it really worth saying? Were you able to show others your passion and your fascination with the image?

It's important to reject a simplistic or superficial rendition of the subject. Instead, find a way of stating your feelings in a more challenging way. When first beginning to make art in any particular medium, mastery of that medium is the first goal; you have to know the basics. So the first pieces you make might be rather wooden as you focus on getting the composition, the colors, and the communication right and believable. But when you have mastery of technique, then you can focus on bringing a fresh response to your own visions.

Flora and Ferra
by Elizabeth Barton
24″ × 45″

Is this a pretty black-and-white design? Are these buildings industrial? Are they operating at the expense of the environment? Look closer!

Mark of the Hand

One of the beauties of an art that grew from a craft is the mark of the hand (page 103), so it is important to avoid a machine-made, overly slick, production look to your work. This can be very difficult at times, such as if you're working with digital photographs printed onto cloth—it may be hard to stitch into grandma's head, but it's important to make this a handmade piece. The mark of the hand can be conveyed in the way that you draw or cut your lines or in the stitching that you add. If everything's too rigid, it detracts from the work. It's important that the viewer (and hopefully collector) can see that a real, living, thinking, feeling person made the work.

Good Technique

Poor technique detracts, but traditional quilt judges often placed too much emphasis on length of stitches and neatness of binding, probably because it's difficult to be objective about an abstract concept such as design. Technique is more easily assessed. It *is* important but *only* insofar as it supports the idea and does not detract from it. It is a means to an end, not the whole point. A piece should go beyond technique, craftsmanship, and presentation.

Energy

Electric Fields
by Elizabeth Barton
45˝ × 34˝

Half of my friends hated *Electric Fields*, and half loved it—strong emotions are good!

Photo by Karen J. Hamrick

A piece that has energy and tension will often create discord among the viewers. Consider the work of artists such as Tracey Emin (you can find her work on the Internet). It's very edgy and self-involved. She's quite fearless in her revelations about her thoughts and feelings. You might not like the work, but it engages you. Her message is loud and crude but also unanticipated as it is conveyed in the soft medium of fabric stitched neatly onto blankets. Her misspellings (she's dyslexic, though she has an MA in painting from the Royal College of Art) make you read every word and hear her voice.

They're unexpected. This is the kind of fiber work that is noticed in the art world. I'm not necessarily suggesting you emulate it, but be aware of two things: (1) the power of the unexpected, and (2) the kind of art that is strong in the art world right now. People wonder why fiber isn't accepted by museums and think maybe it's because it's traditionally women's work or that there is a prejudice against the medium. But I think the reality is that traditional work in *any* medium is not of interest to the current art world unless it is truly top-notch *or* very unexpected and startling.

Good from a Distance, Better Closeup

A strong art quilt works at every distance. From afar, the strong overall design stands out; as you approach the piece, the details and colors begin to draw you in; and up close, you are enthralled by the surface texture and all the exciting little discoveries to be made.

LEARNING FROM JURORS' STATEMENTS

If you are particularly interested in getting your work into shows, read catalogs, jurors' statements, and any reviews that you can. Find the people who see and judge a lot of artwork—learning what they think can be very helpful. For example, when discussing the criteria for choosing art for an exhibit, David Levy, former president and director of the Corcoran Gallery (Washington, D.C.), wrote: "It is important to try to understand what an artist is attempting to accomplish and then evaluate the degree to which the objective is achieved."

Levy went on to state that visual art should be about communicating complex emotions, ideas, and thoughts in a way that words cannot.

Too often both jurors and viewers come to their task with too narrow a perspective. What's chosen or closely observed should *not* be just what they like. When listening to people talk about a quilt show and how the jurors have chosen the work, there seems to be a controversy related to the different weights given to the technical expertise of the work versus the freshness and liveliness and meaningfulness of the content of the piece. This is a balance that each individual jury panel has to settle within themselves and also within the wishes of the organization hosting the show. Overall, the best work should embody both, so often an expert mastery of technique kills the spark. You must make your own judgment on that, but I feel that the concept of *shibui* (page 103) clearly points the way. In nature, would the "perfect" tree be one that had no occasional misshaped leaves, no traces of insects or birds having visited it, no odd quirks, no marks of the life it has lived bending toward the light and shifting in the wind? Think about it!

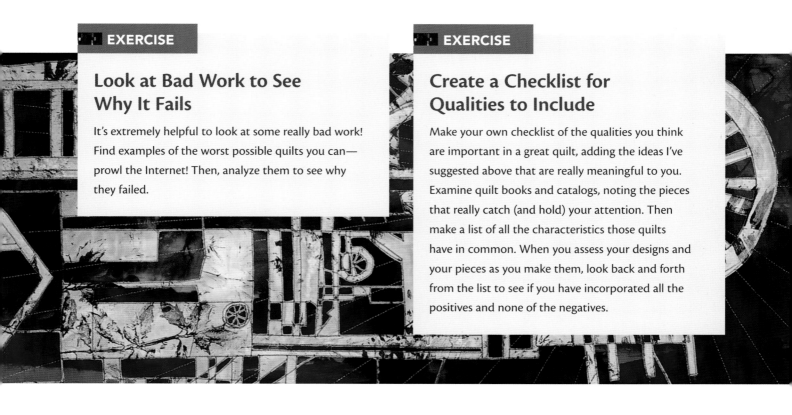

EXERCISE

Look at Bad Work to See Why It Fails

It's extremely helpful to look at some really bad work! Find examples of the worst possible quilts you can— prowl the Internet! Then, analyze them to see why they failed.

EXERCISE

Create a Checklist for Qualities to Include

Make your own checklist of the qualities you think are important in a great quilt, adding the ideas I've suggested above that are really meaningful to you. Examine quilt books and catalogs, noting the pieces that really catch (and hold) your attention. Then make a list of all the characteristics those quilts have in common. When you assess your designs and your pieces as you make them, look back and forth from the list to see if you have incorporated all the positives and none of the negatives.

A checklist should not be used like a recipe, but rather as a way of assessing the strength and beauty of your quilt. After brainstorming uncritically and freely a lot of different design ideas, take out your checklist and run your eye over it. As you begin to block out the quilt on the design wall, take a break from time to time to contemplate it. I like to do this at the beginning and end of each session so that I can see how the idea is progressing. I ask myself: Does everything look right? Is it interesting? Any sore thumbs? Good rhythms? And so on through the list. Eventually these assessments will become second nature and your instincts and intuition will develop.

Here's the list that Dominie Nash, Sue Pierce, Karen Perrine, and I once put together:

1. What was my very first impression from across the gallery?

2. As I drew closer, was there more to see and interest me?

3. As I stood right next to the piece, were there yet more discoveries and delights?

4. How does this piece make me feel? Does it make a strong impression?

5. What mood or message is the artist conveying? What does the piece communicate? How well is the meaning conveyed?

6. Will I remember this piece? Will I enjoy revisiting it in my memory? Why will I remember it?

7. How would this piece look hanging in my living room? What would it add to the room?

8. How would it work in a public space?

9. How long will it stay fresh, interesting, even intriguing, if I look at it every day?

10. How does it relate to the art or art quilt world in general?

11. Which areas are really striking? And do these sections relate to the overall meaning of the work?

12. Are there any parts of it that are not successful, and why?

13. Squinting my eyes to see the value pattern: Is it integrated? Is it interesting? Is it strong?

14. Is this piece unified, or are any elements odd, distracting, out of place, or unnecessary?

15. Is it all extremely predictable, or are there areas of tension, freshness, and new validity?

16. Is everything in balance and in proportion?

17. Are interesting rhythms depicted in some of the basic elements?

END NOTE

Think about all the topics I have raised in this chapter; make a note on your design wall of the key points that you feel are particular to your series. For self-critique, I suggest you write down the questions you feel are important when you look at work. Use these when evaluating your own and other people's work, and keep adding to your list as you see and make more work. In this way, not only will your own work become stronger, but your assessment of, and therefore enjoyment of, others' work will grow too.

Keep working on your series! There is but one road to the top: practice, practice, practice.

BIBLIOGRAPHY

Barton, Elizabeth. *Inspired to Design: Seven Steps to Successful Art Quilts.* Lafayette, CA: C&T Publishing, 2013.

Blockley, John. *Country Landscapes in Watercolor.* New York: Watson-Guptill, 1982.

Bothwell, Dorr, and Marlys Mayfield. *Notan: The Dark–Light Principle of Design.* New York: Reinhold Book Corp., 1991.

Carlson, John. *Carlson's Guide to Landscape Painting.* Mineola, NY: Dover Publications Inc., 1973.

Goldsworthy, Andy. *Andy Goldsworthy: A Collaboration with Nature.* Moffat, UK: Cameron & Hollis, 1990

Hockney, David. *Secret Knowledge: Rediscovering the Lost Techniques of the Old Masters.* London: Thames & Hudson, Limited, 2001.

Tharp, Twyla, and Mark Reiter. *The Creative Habit: Learn It and Use It for Life.* New York: Simon & Schuster, 2005

Truitt, Anne. *Daybook: The Journal of an Artist.* New York: Penguin Books, 1984

ABOUT THE AUTHOR

Elizabeth Barton lives in Athens, Georgia, in a house on a hillside surrounded by beautiful trees, which give endless seasonal variety. She grew up in York, England, where she walked to school (one founded in the seventeenth century) along city walls built by the Romans around AD 71.

Seeing every day the effects of time on buildings and landscape influenced her first quilts. Growing up in a dark northern city made light and windows extremely important. Many of her quilts are about light and the contrast between dark and light.

Elizabeth originally trained as a clinical psychologist and pursued this occupation for many years, both in England and in the United States. Gradually, however, the idea of creating art from fabric grew ever more fascinating, and one year she just decided to let the license lapse and pursue art instead. Athens, Georgia, has an active art and music community, offering a lot of encouragement and support from the surface design professors at the university as well as opportunities for solo shows (of which she has had several). She began

teaching at Arrowmont School for Arts and Crafts (Gatlinburg, Tennessee), then wrote lessons for online courses, and finally was persuaded to put everything into books. This is her second book with C&T Publishing.

Please visit her at:

- www.elizabethbarton.com
- www.elizabethbarton.blogspot.com

Also by Elizabeth Barton:

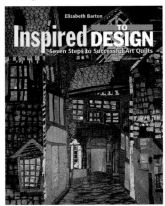

Great Titles and Products

from C&T PUBLISHING

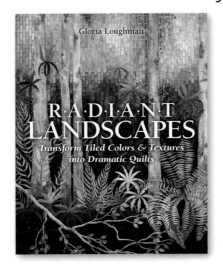

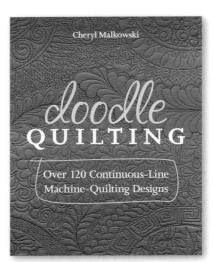

Available at your local retailer or **www.ctpub.com** *or* **800-284-1114**